The Magic Of
Forgiveness

The Magic Of Forgiveness

J. P. VASWANI

Compiled By: Dr. (Mrs.) Prabha Sampath
and Krishna Kumari

New You Books
494 Durie Avenue
Closter, NJ 07624
Tel. No. 201.768.7857
Fax No. 201.768.0433
E-mail: info@newyoubooks.com
www.newyoubooks.com

First published by New You Books 4/13/06

ISBN: 1-4259-3051-4 (sc)

Printed in the United States of America
Bloomington, Indiana

This book is printed on acid-free paper.

Contents

Anger Ceaseth Not By Anger

In the course of a debate in the American Congress, a senator, J. P. Benjamin, made a personal attack on senator W. H. Seward. It lasted for a considerable time. Then Benjamin resumed his seat, angry and bitter, to await a counter-attack.

To the wonder of all present, Senator Seward went over to his opponent and said sweetly, "Benjamin, give me a cigar. When your speech has been printed, send me two copies."

Later, Seward was seen joking with his colleagues, puffing contentedly on the cigar he had received from his opponent.

Anger ceaseth not by anger; anger ceaseth by forgiveness. Forgiveness is, perhaps, the most powerful antidote to anger. Forgiveness and the willingness to be reconciled to those who, for some reason or the other, are not well-disposed towards us. Willingness to be reconciled is all that is needed. For, reconciliation is a two-way process into which a person cannot be forced. I can forgive another but cannot compel the other to forgive me in return.

Forgiveness has been defined as "a process of ceasing to feel resentment against someone or to pardon someone." To cling to resentments is to harm oneself, to walk the way of spiritual death. To choose to let go of resentments is to walk the way that leads to a life of freedom and fulfilment. The person who holds on to anger or resentment is, without his knowing it, causing damage to himself from within. The person who forgives enters a new life of gentle peacefulness. Forgiveness is its own reward. It is the forgiver rather than the forgiven who receives the greater benefit.

Forgiveness acts like magic. Forgiveness provides a magical solution to many of our problems.

Man grows in true greatness in the measure in which he is able to express the quality of forgiveness. All our great ones have been men and women of forgiveness. Even so, forgiveness is not the monopoly of the great. Simple souls, humble men and women have practised the art of forgiveness to perfection.

A house, in which a man and his ten-year-old daughter lived, was attacked by some outlaws. The father died in the scuffle. The outlaws spared the life of the girl, Melania, but gouged out her eyes, so that she became blind. Ten years later, Melania was sitting by the roadside, when she heard footsteps and a voice which frightened her. "Who is it?" she called out, "Be careful, because I am blind."

"I know you are," replied one of the outlaws. "I am the man who killed your father and blinded you. I just tried to hold up a passer-by and he shot me. I am going to die. I beg you to forgive me."

Melania shuddered with anger but controlled herself, forgave the criminal and exhorted him to repent. When the man was dead, she groped for his eyes and gently closed them like a loving daughter.

The French Dauphin, son of Louis XVI, was a prisoner in the hands of a rough jailor, who treated him cruelly, for the crime of having been born as the son of the king.

One day, the jailor asked him, "What would you do with me if the throne was restored to you and you become the King of France? Would you have me hanged?"

The orphan prince simply answered, "I would forgive you!"

It is difficult to imagine what life would be without the spirit of forgiveness. How true it is that, he who has not forgiven an enemy, has never yet tasted one of the most sublime joys of life. Let us forgive one another while there is yet time, for the day cometh when the opportunity to forgive will be taken away from us.

We are told that two of the greatest writers of the nineteenth century, Thackeray and Dickens, became rivals and estranged. Just before Christmas, 1883, they met in London and deliberately failed to recognise each other. Then suddenly, Thackeray turned back, seized the hand of Dickens and said he could no longer bear the coldness that existed between them. Dickens was touched, they parted with smiles. The old jealousy was destroyed.

Almost immediately afterwards, Thackeray suddenly died. What a relief it must have been to Dickens that they had shaken hands so warmly a day or so before! We must not delay in seeking or offering forgiveness. For another opportunity may not be given us to do so.

It was Josh Mcdowell who said, "When I refuse to forgive, I am burning a bridge that someday I will need to pass over."

No negative emotion is ever appeased by indulgence – it demands more and more until it consumes you. So it is with revenge and retaliation. The more you seek them, the more they will lead to hatred, anger and violence.

The Buddha saw that a quarrel had erupted among two factions of his *bikkhus.* The animosity grew until they became virtually irreconcilable. Buddha brought them to their senses with the following story.

Brahmadutta was the King of Benaras. When he conquered his neighbouring kingdom Kaushala, he sought to kill Dirgheti, the King of that country, and his Queen, so that his rule would be secure. However, Dirgheti and his wife made good their escape, going into hiding and living in disguise at the humble dwelling of a potter who was their loyal and devout follower.

In time, they had a son called Dirghayu whom they brought up with loving care. When he was sixteen, he was sent to a Gurukul to complete his education.

When the son was away, Dirgheti and his queen were spotted by a barber who recognised them and betrayed the secret of their presence to Brahmadutta. Determined to destroy his old enemy, Brahmadutta ordered them to be executed.

A large crowd had gathered to witness the execution in Benaras. Among the crowd was Dirghayu, who was shocked and grieved to find that his parents were about to be killed. However, Dirgheti saw him pushing his way through the crowds and gave him a warning shout, "Oh my son, do not look long, do not look short. Hatred is not appeased by hatred, but by non-hatred alone."

That stopped Dirghayu in his tracks, for he realised the wisdom of his father's words. Brahmadutta realised that there was a son somewhere in the crowd, but there was no way he could be spotted. Before the eyes of their son, King Dirgheti and his wife were executed. Dirghayu was devastated and left with a terrible sense of loss and pain.

Years rolled by. Dirghayu became an expert elephant handler and obtained employment in the royal elephant stables. Here he would play the flute in his leisure hours. The King heard the melodious music of the flute and was enchanted by it. He asked to see the young man, and found him to be handsome, virtuous and courteous. He was forthwith appointed as the King's chosen companion and confidant, accompanying him wherever he went.

Little did Brahmadutta realise that the young man whom he held in such affection and trust was the son of the King whom he had executed so ruthlessly. Nor did he know that Dirghayu was just biding time to find the right opportunity of killing him in revenge.

One fine day, that long-awaited opportunity came. Hunting in the forests, Brahmadutta and Dirghayu were separated from the rest of the King's party, as they pursued their quarry. Dirghayu was driving the King's chariot, and they stopped when they realised they had lost the others. So they got down from the chariot. It was a hot day and the King was tired. Dirghayu asked him to lay his head on his lap and go to sleep. The King did so without hesitation, for he trusted the young man absolutely.

Soon he was fast asleep. Dirghayu saw that this was the opportunity he had been waiting for all along. There was no one around, and the King was utterly in his power. Quietly, the young man unsheathed his sword and then, the words of his father flashed across his mind, and he put the sword away.

At the same time, the King was awakened by a terrible dream. He dreamt that the son of the royal couple executed by him, had managed to reach him, and was standing over him with a drawn sword, ready to kill him in vengeance.

As the King narrated this frightening dream, Dirghayu drew his sword again and said, "That was no ordinary dream. It was a warning to you. I am the son you dreamt of, and I am about to kill you in revenge for the death of my parents."

"Please spare my life!" begged the King, holding the young man's hands in despair. "Do not kill me, I beg of you."

"Surely, Oh King, you will have me executed if I spare your life," said Dirghayu. "For you know my identity now, and you will not have me around, as I am the royal heir to the throne of Kaushala. If I don't kill you, I must get killed!"

"Let us then make a pact *not* to kill each other," said the King. "Let this vicious cycle of fear, hatred and vindictiveness be broken forever!"

14

The two pledged lifelong loyalty and friendship. The King, recovering from his traumatising experience, asked Dirghayu to tell him the meaning of his father's intriguing final message.

Dirghayu explained to him, "Do not look long – it means do not nurse your hatred for a long time. Do not look short – this means do not act hastily. If I had acted hastily I would have killed you – only to be killed by your guards when they found us. Then my friends and followers would pursue your people in vengeance and the hatred would continue. However, you and I have extended mutual forgiveness, and therefore both of us can be free of fear. The cycle of violence is now broken."

Concluding the story, the Buddha reminded his disciples that hatred only leads to further hatred, while love and forgiveness can conquer hatred and promote peace.

They who forgive most shall be most forgiven.

Philips J. Bailey

Why Should We Forgive?

The distinguished psychologist, Dr. Richard Johnson, lists the following points as the practical benefits of forgiveness:

- Firstly, it stimulates our spiritual growth – which is stunted, stopped in its tracks by an unforgiving nature. Forgiveness releases us from the deadening burden of resentment and blame and allows us to use our spiritual energy in constructive ways.

- Secondly, the act of forgiveness restores our vitality, stamina and zest for life.

- Thirdly, it restores peace and harmony in our lives.

- Fourthly, it allows us to live a more abundant life, with an uncluttered soul, an unburdened heart and a mind free from resentment and recriminations.

16

Resentment and anger are destructive emotions. They damage us from within and the damage is manifested in symptoms that are almost unbearable – the inability to go to sleep in peace; the gnawing feeling in the pit of the stomach; the heavy burden of sorrow on the heart; the throbbing headache; the blinding pain...

No wonder Emerson wrote, "For every minute you remain angry, you give up sixty seconds of peace of mind."

Forgiveness holds the promise of freedom and relief from such anguish.

Forgiveness offers the chance for reparation, reconciliation and atonement – in some cases, after years of hostility and estrangement.

Kamla and Kishore were siblings. They had enjoyed a loving and caring relationship as children. But in adulthood, after they had married and started their own separate families, they grew apart. Kishore's wife had been disrespectful to Kamla and her mother, and Kamla was angry and upset that her brother did not speak up. The resentment grew until brother and sister were no longer on talking terms. One day, Kamla was surprised to find a letter from Kishore in

17

her mailbox. By now it was six years since they had spoken to each other – even though they lived in the same city. Kishore had written to say that his wife was expecting twins, and they both wanted her to visit them and bless the babies, soon after their birth. He also expressed regret and shame over his long silence, and concluded the letter with the words, "We apologise for whatever it was that we did, which has brought about this estrangement with a sister whom I love dearly."

Kamla had hardly read the letter when she burst out in indignation, "*Whatever it was... whatever it was?* Doesn't he know how shamefully they behaved! Well, I'll tell him!"

She sat down to write a letter in which she poured out all her pent up bitterness, telling him in detail all the sins of omission and commission he was guilty of, and how much she had been hurt by it all. The letter ran to some six pages. As she was about to put it in an envelope, the telephone rang. It was a call from her son's school, asking her to attend an urgent meeting of the PTA. It was several hours before she got back to the letter which she had left on her desk.

When she re-read her letter, she was appalled by her own malice and resentment.

"How could I be so mean and unforgiving?" she asked herself. "I must be the most hard-hearted woman in the world! And surely, it was not all Kishore's fault…" Her eyes misted over with tears of forgiveness and compassion.

Next day, she called up Kishore on the phone. "I am so happy to talk to you again," she told him. "I can't wait to see you both – and I am proud that I am going to be the aunt of twins!"

Kamla discovered that forgiveness set her free!

Forgiveness can make your working environment congenial and smooth.

In any institution or organisation, people of different temperaments and natures come to work together for the common good of their workplace. I have always maintained that the plane of action is also the plane of friction. Misunderstandings and quarrels are sure to crop up, human nature being what it is. When these are borne on the heart as grudges, the working atmosphere is vitiated. If, on the other hand, resentments are forgiven and forgotten, people can continue to work together harmoniously.

19

Forgiveness enables us to sustain and cherish relationships that matter to us. If there are associations in our life that are about to be brought to an end, forgiveness brings them to a painless and hassle-free conclusion, leaving us free to move on!

John Stuart Mill was a great philosopher; Thomas Carlyle was an acclaimed writer. Both men were firm friends. Carlyle was writing his masterpiece *The French Revolution* at that time. Mill asked to see the manuscript, for he was eager to read his friend's work and see what it had to say.

Carlyle willingly gave him the manuscript, inviting Mill to give him his suggestions for improvement.

A few days later, a pale and ashen-faced Mill arrived at Carlyle's door. The writer let him into the study and found that Mill was trembling.

"What is it John?" he asked gently.

"My friend, I hardly know how to begin," stammered the philosopher. "I am so sorry – but your manuscript has been swept away by a careless maid in my house. I shudder to say this – nothing remains of it but a few torn shreds! How can I ever make up to you for this? I apologise, most profusely…"

He broke off, unable to continue.

Carlyle was stunned into silence. But pulling himself together, he said to his friend, "Do sit down John. What has happened has happened. Pray don't blame yourself."

Mill sank into an armchair with a profound sigh. He was so overcome with regret and embarrassment that he stayed there talking to his friend till it was well past midnight. It was the only thing that could relieve him of his acute misery and shock.

Finally, he rose to go. Carlyle laid his hand on his shoulder and said, "Let's look at it this way. It is as if a master has asked his pupil to rewrite an average essay to perfection!"

There was a man who knew how to sustain a valuable friendship through forgiveness!

Actually, as he watched Mill leave his house, considerably chastened but nevertheless relieved by his friend's magnanimity, Carlyle confessed to his wife, "I cannot tell you how crushed I feel by this misfortune. But I did not want him to see it."

Forgiveness brings peace and joy into our life. Forgiveness puts an end to the inner struggle that rages in the soul within, and teaches us to face life with tolerance, understanding and equanimity.

The horrendous Kurukshetra war had just ended. The Kauravas were almost completely wiped out. The victorious Pandavas were closeted with Sri Krishna, discussing the implications of their momentous, yet in some ways, tragic victory.

Sri Krishna told the Pandavas and their sons, who occupied two separate tents, to exchange places for the night.

It was a far-sighted, prophetic suggestion. For later that night, Ashwathama, Duryodana's friend and the son of Dronacharya, stole into the Pandava camp on a deadly mission to avenge his slain father and friend. He swooped into what he thought was the tent of the Pandavas, and massacred all Draupadi's sons.

When the distraught mother learnt of the heinous crime, her anguish and anger were beyond control.

Arjuna sought out Ashwathama, vanquished him in single combat and dragged the defeated warrior before his disconsolate wife.

For a moment, murderous hatred flashed in Draupadi's tear-filled eyes – but only for a moment.

She sobered down. It seemed as if she had no more tears to shed. Slowly, she said to Arjuna, "Do not kill him *Aryaputra*. Let him be spared…let not another mother suffer the bereavement of her child!"

A grievously wronged mother, Draupadi was able to put an end to the struggle that raged within her soul between revenge and forgiveness!

Forgiveness frees us from guilt and self-loathing. It liberates us from the constricting feeling that others are controlling our emotional reactions and dictating our attitudes.

A staff meeting was being held at a school. The head master invited suggestions from the teachers for improving the performance of the students in the examinations.

A young and enthusiastic maths teacher said, "Let us announce that all students who score over 85% will be given a full refund of the examination fees."

There was a heated reaction to this suggestion. "Ridiculous", "idiotic", "impractical" were some of the remarks made by senior teachers.

The young staff member was not offended. He smiled and said, "I'm sorry that you are not able to see the pragmatism of my suggestion. You must surely realise what a tremendous incentive it will be for students to perform well and claim their refund!"

The head master was so impressed with the young man's enthusiasm that he decided to implement the suggestion. How different the situation would have been if the young teacher had been hurt by the adverse remarks and decided to stop contributing to the discussions!

When you blame other people for your reactions, when you believe they are responsible for your feelings, you relinquish control over your life. You allow others to take charge. You become a passive victim.

Don't let others control your feelings! When you realise that you are the master of your own emotions, when you assume the responsibility for your own feelings, you begin to react very differently. You learn to overcome negative feelings, you learn to walk away from disappointments and hurts without being broken or embittered.

Forgiveness raises our self-esteem by making us aware of our own potential for goodness, love and compassion.

Forgiveness enables us to live at peace with ourselves and others, free from emotional strife.

In short, forgiveness transforms our life, making it more peaceful, meaningful and constructive.

There is also a very rational and practical need for us to forgive. When we have been hurt or ill-treated or injured by someone, we can choose either to retaliate or to forgive and forget. If we choose to retaliate, we will allow ourselves to be consumed by resentment. For revenge does not leave us happy; it leaves us feeling empty and embittered. Has anyone ever heard of anger being satisfied? But forgiveness, as I said, is pragmatic. It allows us to put an end to all the unpleasantness and to get on with the vital act of living the rest of our lives in peace.

There is a Chinese proverb which says, whoever opts for vengeance should dig two graves.

An unforgiving attitude is deadly. It destroys the offender and the offended. On the other hand, forgiveness is the key to peace and happiness.

> Without forgiveness life is governed by an endless cycle of resentment and retaliation.
>
> *Anon.*

What Is Forgiveness?

There is no easy or simple way to define forgiveness. Forgiveness is a bridge that all of us need to cross at one time or another in our lives. Forgiveness is an act of will which we have to carry out consciously and deliberately. Forgiveness is an attitude of compassion and understanding with which we choose to react to the world. Forgiveness is not a one-off action – it is a *process* by which we evolve towards tolerance and acceptance. Forgiveness is not a series of incidents – it is a way of life that we choose. Forgiveness is self-restraint, self-control, self-discipline, through which we transcend our lower selves. Above all, forgiveness is an effort on our part to bring out the divine that is in all of us.

Forgiveness is not always easy. How can parents forgive the murderers of their children? How can mothers forgive the rapists of their daughters? How can anyone forgive those who have massacred their family and friends?

I am the first to admit it is not easy. But the alternative is to become *like* those offenders – intransigent, cruel and unfeeling. Forgiveness releases you from the fetters of hatred, and frees you from the pain, shame and humiliation of the past which is, thankfully, dead and gone!

Are there no limits to forgiveness? Would forgiveness not mean exonerating, excusing, or condoning evil actions? Would this not be immoral, not to speak of it being unethical and unjust?

The writer and poet C. S. Lewis argues that forgiveness transcends the idea of human fairness. It sometimes involves pardoning those things that can't be pardoned at all. It is much more than excusing. When we excuse someone, we simply brush their mistakes aside. As he puts it, "If one was not really to blame, then there is nothing to forgive. In that sense forgiveness and excusing are almost opposites." He concludes:

> Real forgiveness means looking steadily at the sin, the sin that is left over without any excuse, after all allowances have been made, and seeing

it in all its horror, dirt, meanness, and malice, and nevertheless being wholly reconciled to the person who has done it. That and only *that* is forgiveness.

Even when reconciliation is not possible, forgiveness can play a vital role. George Macdonald writes:

It may be infinitely worse to refuse to forgive than to murder, because the latter may be the impulse of a moment of heat, whereas the former is a cold and deliberate choice of the heart.

Forgiveness need not be a struggle – if we realise that it is also a great gift and a blessing. It is a choice that we make – either to love or hate, to punish or pardon, to heal or hurt. We choose to tread the path of peace and reconciliation, rather than succumb to bitterness. To quote the words of Martin Luther King, Jr., "Forgiveness is not an occasional act. It is a permanent attitude."

Forgiveness is above justice. Justice seeks to punish, forgiveness seeks reconciliation. As Shakespeare puts it so beautifully:

Though justice be thy plea, consider this:
That in the course of justice none of us should see salvation.
We do pray for mercy

And that same prayer doth teach us all to render
The deeds of mercy.

Forgiveness is not only for saints and sages. How often have we not come across people, who, when urged to forgive and forget, will retort with passion, "I am not a *mahatma*...I am not a saint... I am only human!"

So many of us believe that we cannot forgive; that it is too difficult, that it is the prerogative of saints and other evolved souls and not for the likes of us.

Forgiveness need not be a feat of supernatural power. It is just a way of putting the past behind you, once and for all. It is a way of moving on. It is a way of seeing things differently, looking at life from a new perspective. It is the realisation that we cannot stay bitter and angry for the rest of our lives.

Forgiveness is the noblest virtue. Here is a story to illustrate this. A rich old man divided all his property equally among his sons. However, he withheld an expensive diamond ring, which was a family heirloom. His sons were being sent out to travel and take on the world. When they returned on a certain specified day, the diamond ring would go to him who had done the noblest deed.

On the appointed day the sons returned home. They were asked to report on what they considered to be their noblest deed.

The first son said, "A wealthy banker handed over all his money to me for investment. I could have kept it all – but I served him honestly, and restored every pie of his to him, with interest."

"That was indeed well done – but you only did what you should do," said the father.

The second son said, "As I was walking along the seashore, I saw a little child who was about to drown. At the risk of my life, I rushed into the roaring waves and rescued the child."

"That was a brave deed – but not worthy enough to deserve the priceless ring!" was the father's response.

It was the youngest son's turn. "I was tending my sheep on the mountains, when I saw my bitterest enemy stumble on the edge of a precipice and fall. He hung on to the edge of the cliff in terror – I rushed to his aid and saved his life!"

"You are my pride and joy," said the father. "Returning good for evil is the noblest deed. The ring shall be yours!"

Forgiveness Is An Act Of Will

Forgiveness is a deliberate and conscious choice that we make. It cannot come out of compulsion or pressure.

Two women working in an organisation got into a bitter quarrel over who should be given the use of the new laptop in their departments. Heated words led to arguments, arguments turned into acrimony – and then to anger and resentment. Soon, they were not on talking terms.

The team leader was dismayed at the turn of events. He felt that this would affect the cohesive functioning of the team, and invited both the women to come into his office. Perhaps they could sort things out over a cup of coffee.

They arrived in his office and sat stiffly, ignoring each other, even refusing to look at each other. They stared straight at his face when he made his fervent appeal to them – to rise above their differences, to let bygones be bygones. It was important for them as individuals to be on friendly terms with the other members of the team. It was vital for the organisation, that everyone got on well and worked in unity and amity.

As the younger woman listened, she saw the good sense of what her boss was saying. Soon, she softened, and began to nod in agreement with his words. "True," she said every now and then, "I see your point," or "I guess I agree with you."

At the same time, she also began to turn towards her colleague, with an occasional smile and a friendly glance.

However, the older woman continued to be stiff and unbending. She neither smiled, nor spoke, but continued to stare at the boss. She remained rigid and frozen, refusing to allow the earnest appeals of the boss to influence her.

He finished his delicate task and turned to look at both women, "What do you have to say, ladies?" he asked them both.

The younger one spoke up at once. "You are perfectly right sir," she said. "I am sorry I allowed my ill-temper to run away with me. I assure you it won't happen again. I won't let anything interfere with the work of the organisation."

Turning to her colleague, she extended her hand, saying, "Please forgive me, Barbara. It was wrong of me to get so worked up over a little thing like a laptop. I do apologise!"

The older woman ignored the proffered hand. In fact she did not even look at the other but said coldly to the boss, "I am afraid I cannot compromise my beliefs for the asking. I have done no wrong, and I have no intention of resuming my association with someone whom I can't put up with. This is a personal matter, and you have no right to tell me how to deal with my personal business."

Forgiveness is flexibility. It allows you to react to changing situations instead of being rigid and intransigent.

It requires maturity, wisdom and sensitivity to look at ourselves and others dispassionately, objectively. It requires courage to overcome the ego that tells us that we can do no wrong, and that it is the others who are at fault.

Forgiveness is an attitude of compassion and understanding with which we choose to react to the world around us. We stop seeing others as insensitive and unfeeling or rude and boorish, or cold and selfish. We try to understand their weaknesses, their fear and insecurity, which made them behave in a way that hurt us. In a sense, it is a scared, confused and hurt child inside each one of us which is responsible for such outbursts. This child lurks even within the adult, getting out of hand at times.

At such times, it may be our first impulse to react with, "How dare you..." or "How *could* you..." But when we realise the other person's problems, we gain an insight and understanding into their personality. We learn to change our perception and attitude, and this makes forgiveness easy!

Forgiveness is not a one-off action. It is a constant and ongoing process. Mistakes and rash judgements occur again and again in our life. Sometimes we bear the brunt of others' wrongdoing; occasionally, *we* wrong others. Each time this situation occurs, we need to change our attitude, change our perception and move beyond our habitual prejudices. Each time we make this shift in perspective, we grow in the spirit of understanding and compassion, until forgiveness is no longer a difficult and painful business!

Forgiveness is not a series of events wherein we assume the role of misunderstood martyrs gritting our teeth and forgiving others till we are choked by the stress and strain of it all. Forgiveness becomes our habitual approach, a way of life that makes a difference to us and others. We then cease to regard ourselves as persecuted victims. We cease to regard others as insensitive monsters. The realisation dawns that all of us are human – and though we err, stumble and fall, we can always pick ourselves up, dust ourselves off, and get on with our lives. Ultimately, this will enable us to experience the welcome feeling that we are in control of our emotions and reactions; that we are in charge of our own life, and that we can create our own joy and peace and harmony, without having to depend on others to do it for us. Thus we are also released from the helpless dependency syndrome which drives us to expect perfection from others.

We must examine our own attitude to forgiveness consciously and deliberately, to determine what it means to us. Think of someone who has wronged you or hurt you. What does it mean for you to forgive her? What would it take – what would you have to do to forgive?

Forgiveness is not martyrdom. Forgiveness is not self-congratulatory or superior. Unfortunately many of us cling to wrong and absurd notions of forgiveness.

Forgiveness does not mean putting up with unacceptable behaviour. We see so much injustice around us – violence, hatred, abuse, exploitation, and dishonesty. In such cases, you may have to take firm and decisive action, to ensure that the injustice is brought to an end.

It is said that a judge's job is the toughest. He has to abide by the rule of the law, above the feelings of kindness or cruelty.

Justice Charuchandra Dutt faced a terrible dilemma. It was the end of what the lawyers call 'an open-and-shut case.' All evidence pointed to the fact that the accused was indeed guilty. He had killed a man in cold blood, and had to be punished for it.

Justice Dutt, known for his impartial and firm judgement was himself on trial, for the accused was none other than his only son. The sentence was to be delivered on the morrow.

"Save our son!" sobbed his wife, as the Judge sat in reflection. "You can and you must save him! I cannot bear to see him condemned to die at his father's hands."

The Justice laid his hand on his grieving spouse. He had no words to comfort her. How could he make her understand that justice could not be subverted?

Next morning, the judgement was delivered. The guilty young man was to die by hanging.

Having delivered the sentence, the Justice met the prisoner outside the court. He embraced him with tear-filled eyes and murmured, "May God forgive you," and left without a backward glance.

Within minutes of reaching home, Justice Dutt died of a massive cardiac arrest.

Forgiveness is not hypocrisy, forgiveness does not mean deceiving yourself and others. Some of us put on an impassive or cool front, while we are seething with rage inside. Repression is self-destructive, and can lead to psychological problems, for we push aside our genuine feelings and replace them with what we consider to be 'acceptable' feelings. We try to be 'nice' on the outside, when all hell is breaking loose inside us.

A young woman married the only son of a domineering, possessive mother. For the first few years of her marriage, she faced tremendous problems adjusting to a crusty, short-tempered mother-in-law, who could never see anything good in her. But she did not protest or grumble. She just carried on, impassive and sullen.

Five years later, the mother-in-law suffered a severe paralytic stroke. She was confined to bed, unable to walk, talk or move. It was a cruel blow to a proud and strong woman. A nurse and attendant were appointed to care for her, for the family could afford this and more.

The stricken woman lay in her bed, all day long, tears flowing from her eyes constantly.

As for her daughter-in-law, a strange transformation came over her. No longer did she have to play the role of the silent docile daughter-in-law.

Left in charge of the household, she spewed venom and hatred on the mother-in-law, whenever they were alone in each other's presence. Sometimes she would utter harsh words of abuse, sometimes she would poke fun at the mother-in law's helpless condition; sometimes she would treat her with utter disrespect and contempt. But in the presence of others, the impassive mask was back in its place.

The young woman was causing greater psychological damage to herself by her hypocrisy, rather than hurting her mother-in-law, who, in any case, was past the stage of retaliating! I dare say the older woman would have healed inwardly, while the younger woman would be inflicting irreparable wounds on her own psyche!

Forgiveness is not self-righteous. It does not co-exist with an attitude of superiority or condescension.

Consider this situation. A young and inexperienced clerk has typed a report on her first day at work. The report is taken in to the boss for his approval and is found to be full of mistakes. The boss calls the new recruit in and yells abuses at her, berating her for her inefficiency and incompetence.

Trembling in every limb, the clerk stammers an apology, begging the boss to bear with her just once, and promising that it would never happen again.

The man's ego is appeased. He throws the report at her with a dismissive, "Get out of my office, and don't show your face here until the report is perfect! I'm letting you off this time – but that's only because I'm magnanimous!"

Such an attitude demoralises the victim who is at the receiving end – and it does no good to the 'magnanimous' oppressor!

Sometimes we make choices or adopt attitudes that we confuse with forgiveness. Forgiveness is not running away from yourself and your true feelings. Forgiveness is not reducing yourself to an unresponsive, dullened state. True forgiveness is not possible until you are completely honest with yourself.

> I can forgive, but I cannot forget is only another way of saying, I cannot forgive.
>
> *Henry Ward Beecher*

Forgiveness Is Divine

We have all heard of the saying "To err is human, to forgive divine." The goal of our human life is to grow in perfection, to seek to become divine.

Forgiveness – *kshama* – is indeed a divine virtue. It exists in all of us. What we need to do is to allow it to unfold and express itself in deeds of daily living.

There is an interesting story narrated to us in the *Puranas.* Rishi Brighu was overwhelmed by the desire to find out who, among the Holy Trinity of Brahma, Shiva and Vishnu, should be worshipped as the greatest. The sage decided that *He* would be the greatest, who showed the greatest degree of forbearance and forgiveness.

Having formed his plan, Brighu made his way to the abode of Lord Brahma. Having arrived in the presence of the Lord, Brighu simply ignored Him, not touching His feet or bowing before Him, refusing even to acknowledge His presence.

41

Lord Brahma was incensed. He grew incandescent with rage and rose to pronounce a terrible curse on the sage. However, he was restrained by his divine consort Saraswati who said to him, "Dear Lord, please bear with Brighu this once. There must be some reason for his strange behaviour."

Lord Brahma relented, and sage Brighu made a safe escape. His next stop was at Mount Kailash, the abode of Lord Shiva.

Approaching the Lord who sat in divine meditation, Brighu began a tirade. "Look at you!" he laughed scornfully. "Your body is smeared with ashes and you are garlanded by snakes! You must be mad!"

Lord Shiva would have hurled his *trishul* at Brighu in divine wrath, if Mata Parvati had not held him back, saying, "Let him go, my Lord, just once!" Shiva was loath to let him go – but allowed him to flee, for the sake of His beloved wife.

Fleeing for his life from Kailash, he went to Vaikunth, where Lord Vishnu, the Great Preserver of the Universe lay in his divine *yoganidra.* Emboldened by the peaceful sleep of the Lord, Brighu did what was unimaginable – he kicked the Lord in the chest, and shouted, "How can you go off to sleep, without a care for your task of sustaining life in this world?"

Lord Vishnu awoke.

The moment he opened his eyes, Lord Vishnu clutched the feet of the sage. "Forgive me, O Holy one!" He pleaded. "Your holy, sacred foot must surely have been hurt by the hardness of my chest! How can I soothe the pain that I have inadvertently caused to you – one of my greatest devotees?"

His eyes, filled with unbidden tears, Brighu fell at the Lotus feet of the Lords. "Forgive my arrogance and folly," he pleaded, "for I set out to judge you! O Lord of supreme compassion, how will I ever wash away the terrible sin of having kicked your holy chest? What a great shame and disrepute will come on my head!"

"How can any father be angry with the infant who kicks his chest?" said the Lord, smiling. "You are my loving son, and you have taken a child's liberty with your Father. Your footprint shall remain imprinted on my chest, for ages to come."

Such is the power of divine forgiveness!

People often relate this story to argue about the superiority of one God over another. I think they lose the whole point of this parable from the *Puranas*. It is meant to reinforce the power of divine forgiveness. If the Lord Himself can forgive such a heinous offence, who are we to nurse grudges against our fellow human beings?

There is no revenge so complete as forgiveness.

Anon.

Forgiveness cannot change the past, but it can enlarge the future.

Anon.

Hatred is a fire which keeps burning within the heart : it burns away all your happiness.

– J. P. Vaswani

Forgiveness Is Power

In his immortal Sermon on the Mount, Jesus Christ exhorts us to love our enemies and bless those who persecute us. He practised what he preached too! All of us thrill to his message of ultimate forgiveness when he was breathing his last, crucified to death, "O Lord, forgive them, for they know not what they do."

Love your enemies. Bless those who persecute you. This is not empty rhetoric – these are not just tall words. I say this to you, because many people are dismissive of this attitude. They regard this advice as weak, cowardly, foolish and defeatist. And besides, how can we love and bless those who wish to destroy us?

"Probably no admonition of Jesus has been more difficult to follow than the command to love your enemies," wrote Martin Luther King Jr. in his bestseller, *Strength To Love* "...Far from being the

45

pious injunction of a Utopian dreamer, the command to love one's enemy is an absolute necessity for our survival. Love even your enemies – is the key to the solution of the problems of this world."

During the U.S. Civil Rights Movement of the 1960's led by Martin Luther King, several white Americans were targeted for sympathising with the blacks. A white Boston clergyman, James Reed, was beaten up by white protestors, later dying of his injuries. A white woman of Detroit was shot and killed, because she gave a black man a lift in her car.

Students of a small town called Selma in Alabama, took out a peaceful march against these incidents. The march took place after school hours. When the town's notorious, racist Sheriff heard about the march, he set his men on the children in a most cruel and inhuman way. They pushed and prodded the children, forcing them to run until many of the children were sick and retching. The Sheriff's cruel explanation was just this – that he wanted to cure the children of their "marching fever."

A few days later, the Sheriff was hospitalised with severe angina. The same school children whom he had treated so brutally, organised a second Peace

March outside the hospital – chanting prayers for his speedy recovery, and carrying get-well-soon placards.

We live in a society which emphasises ruthless power to succeed. We glorify individualism and the instinct for self-preservation. The act of forgiveness, the attitude of pardon is often regarded as a weakness – even a sign of cowardice. We are told repeatedly: fight for your rights; protect your rights; do not yield to anyone!

I would like to tell you that the act of forgiveness holds great power – not just spiritual power, but the kind of power no one can despise. It asserts your dignity and self-worth. It reveals your inner strength and establishes your ability to forgive. So far from leaving you weak and vulnerable, forgiveness can empower you to lead a more meaningful life. It brings conflicts and struggles to a positive ending – for it helps us to overcome the vicious cycle of resentment and revenge and enter the realms of unity, peace and harmony. What is more important, each act of forgiveness inspires others to do the same, setting off a positive chain reaction.

Forgiveness frees us from remaining victims of the past. It teaches us new ways to respond to events and people. Above all, we can practise forgiveness even against people who have betrayed our faith in human nature – because it frees us from the burden of expectation, of wanting anything in return.

Forgiveness could change the history of modern civilisation if only we allow it to flow through the sea of humanity. Alas, it is we who stand in its way – we refuse to give in, we refuse to let go! Martin Luther King saw forgiveness as having the potential to turn an enemy into a friend. It can transform the world – if only we let its magic work!

Let us forgive one another while there is yet time : for the day cometh when the opportunity to forgive will be taken away from us.

J. P. Vaswani

Forgiveness Can Heal You!

In an inspiring article entitled, "Forgive, Forget and Live", Norman Vincent Peale shares with us the story of a man who seemed to possess the great secret of living positively at all times. He had made St. Paul's great words the motto of his life, "Forgetting those things which are behind, and reaching forth unto those things which are before, I press toward the mark for the prize of the high calling of God…"

Harbouring an unforgiving attitude, nursing resentment and grudges can actually cause illness and disease. A survey conducted in New York revealed that 70% of patients who came to their doctors for treatment, revealed one form or other of resentment in their lives. Looking at their case histories, a well-known physician remarked, "Ill-will and grudges often make people sick. Forgiveness will do more toward getting them well than many pills."

'Grudgitis' is a terrible illness which can even cause death – if a person holds hatred in his heart against another for long. The moral of the story: forgiveness is not only the right way to live, it is also the healthy way to live!

I hear that rich, fashion-conscious women often undergo what is called 'wart-removal' or 'blemish-removal' surgeries to make themselves beautiful. Dr. Peale recommends what he calls a "resentment removal" job on ourselves! And he suggests preliminary steps to achieve this 'self-beautification' surgery:

1. Be firm and determined to rid yourself of resentment – no matter how tough it is, no matter how long it takes.

2. Don't forget the great harm that resentment can do to your system. It may even kill you!

3. Realise that practising forgiveness is the first step on the path of spiritual evolution. Goodwill must flow out of you, so that it can flow back into your life.

4. Don't just *think* about forgiving – actually practise it. Forgive your enemies NOW.

5. Pray for yourself – as well as for the other person. Send positive thoughts to him. Invoke God's blessings on him – and ask for God's forgiveness and blessings on yourself.

6. Talk about the other person in kind terms. This will help get rid of your bitterness.

7. Reach out to the person you resent – through a kind gesture, an action or even a letter. This will also have a cleansing effect.

8. Analyse the factors that caused this 'resentment-pattern' to set in your life. This will help you make sure that the mistakes of the past are not repeated.

The truth is that a troubled conscience will never allow us to live in peace and quiet – and our conscience will continue to remain troubled unless we rid ourselves of the hatred and resentment that makes us unforgiving.

George Shinn writes, "We get what we give. If we give hatred, we receive hatred, if we give love, we receive love!"

If we wish to achieve inner peace, there is only one way – release ourselves from anger and resentment, learn to let go of hatred, and practise forgiveness.

Psychiatrists tell us that when people refuse to forgive and forget, their life takes a definite turn for the worse – a downturn. They become bitter and wallow in self-pity. Some become passive, lethargic and bored with life. They stop seeking the company of positive, helpful people and lock themselves up in a prison of isolation and alienation. Some of them, sadly, take to drink. Others find that smoking makes them relax. Thus begins the spiral downwards...

The truth is, if you are unable to forgive and forget, you pay the price in physical and emotional terms. What form this emotional, physical deprivation may take, it is difficult to predict.

A divorced wife who was unable to forgive her husband, developed a cancerous growth which led to surgery. She was convinced that her emotional hurt and resentment had contributed to her cancer.

A Christian pastor who had led a healthy and active life all along, was suddenly taken ill and admitted to the hospital. The doctors found two large polyps (growths) that were infected, and were causing severe pain. They were removed in an emergency surgery. The pastor was convinced that the polyps were the result of the grudge and resentment he bore against two men, whom he could not forgive. Otherwise, they had no reason to be there! Surgery had removed the polyps physically. He now became determined to remove the 'polyps' of hatred from his soul, by developing an attitude of love and forgiveness towards the men he had hated so much in the past.

Medical experts tell us that anger accelerates our ageing process. Anger is indeed a very natural human reaction – and it is a *mature emotion* when we don't allow it to last very long, and when it does not hurt anyone. But if we let anger remain in the heart within, it ceases to be mature and natural – it festers into a grudge. When we refuse to forgive people, we are letting our grudge control our life.

Anger held in the heart within, gnaws us from the inside, wears us down, operating like a poisonous waste that has seeped into our system. This leads us to a state of permanent stress – in a complex 'fight or flight' syndrome.

The fight or flight pattern of behaviour was suited to our primitive ancestor, the cave man. When he encountered a wild animal he had to choose one of two options – stay and fight the animal, if that was manageable, or take to his heels and flee, in order to save his life.

When we are nursing a grudge constantly, we get into this primitive 'fight or flight' situation. We are in a continuous state that prompts us either to attack – give vent to our anger – or just escape from an unbearable situation. This can be extremely harmful to our nervous system. Our physical, emotional, psychological and spiritual energies are so stressed, that we slip into a condition of overall lethargy. This accelerates the ageing process. In this sense anger is the extreme opposite of what was called the fountain of youth. One therapist I read calls it 'The Tub of Ageing.'

Holding on to anger and resentment can also tax our immune system, according to some doctors. Our immune system is a complex assemblage of several parts, processes and healing procedures, say these therapists. This complex system responds to stimuli from within and without. Even a relatively minor ailment, like a cold, can challenge the system and put it on high alert. Outside events like a traffic holdup, a child's stubborn behaviour, the harsh temper of a superior, or a quarrel with your spouse, can have an adverse impact on our immune system.

It has been said that holding a grudge has a destructive effect on one's soul. But I wish to warn you that it can destroy the body too. We all know that stress causes insomnia – but so can bitterness! Research has even revealed a relationship between unresolved anger and cardiac arrest. People who hold grudges fall easy prey to illness and disease. When they make the conscious decision to cease hatred and resentment – they set themselves on the road to recovery. This is why hatred has been likened to cancer – it is the cancer of bitterness that destroys both body and soul.

We still can't explain or even understand how the body-mind-soul connection works. But there is a vast amount of documented research which links the working of the body with the thoughts and feelings of the mind. Our emotional turmoil is manifested in our body. We begin to be at war with ourselves. Doctors have a peculiar word – *to somaticize*. It simply means taking an emotional issue and unconsciously displacing it on to our own body. The result can be anything from a perforated ulcer to a cancerous growth!

Doctors and counsellors at the CMC Hospital, Vellore, have carried out research on patients to prove that several physical ailments are directly related to emotional root causes. Resentment, unforgiveness, hostility, guilt, anger, and enmity cause diseases related to heart, lungs, chest, stomach, intestines, ear, nose, and throat.

These researches show that repressed resentment, anger and unforgiveness lead to definite problems in the organs of digestion, as well as in the head, eyes and ears. These negative emotions are "bottled up" inside us, and we keep "swallowing" their toxic contents, until they affect our health.

Mary Chandler narrates a moving story about the healing power of forgiveness from her own life. When Mary was barely 16 years old, disaster struck her family. A terrible accident took place outside their home, when a huge truck rammed into her parents' car. Her six year old sister and two year old brother were scared stiff, but safe in the back seat. The father was badly shaken, but unharmed. However, her mother was severely injured. Her head lay on the

56

pavement, her feet were still wedged in the car, and blood streamed down her face and hair.

Shocked and terrified, Mary could only pray, "Please God, O please don't let my Mom die!"

In a daze, she watched the ambulance arrive and take her mother away to hospital. Then she saw the driver of the truck – tall, slim, dressed in working clothes – standing with his head bowed, near the smashed car.

"I'm sorry," he said to her. "I'm so sorry, I didn't see the stop sign and ...."

"I hate you!" cried Mary. "I hate you! Look what you've done to my Mom! Why couldn't you drive more carefully? I'll never ever forgive you – I hope God doesn't either!"

Mary was deeply troubled, sorely embittered. What has my Mom done to deserve this, she thought. What have we done to deserve this? Why had God allowed this to happen to them?

"The accident ended my childhood," Mary was to write later. At sixteen, she became the surrogate mother to her siblings – all six of them. The older children shared the chores of cooking, cleaning and laundry with her. She attended school during the day and worked part time in a local movie theatre in the evenings. She did her homework between 11.00 p.m. and 1.00 a.m. at night.

She missed her mother! Her love and warmth and care were all lost to the children. Money was tight too – for her mother's income was now lost. The children could not even visit her as often as they liked, for she had been shifted to a hospital 200 miles away to receive specialised care.

As the weeks dragged on, Mary's bitterness grew. Reports from the hospital were not good – her mother's mind and memory were still hazy. Doctors had still not been able to relieve the pressure on her head.

Mary no longer blamed God for what had happened – but she hated and despised the truck driver who had caused the accident. "*He* should be the one to suffer – not us," she thought in anger.

Her father travelled by bus to visit the hospital whenever he could find time from his overworked and underpaid job. As for the children, they were allowed to talk to their mother once every few weeks, whenever she could find the strength to talk – even that seemed to exhaust her.

Worries, responsibilities and constant work took their toll on the children. One night, Mary was sitting at the dining table, working on a huge pile of assignments, when she was overwhelmed by tears. "I can't go on like this," she sobbed. "God, please help me." She felt the old bitterness and anger return, as she thought of the tall, thin truck driver.

" Mary," she heard her mother's voice saying, " I have forgiven him. It's time you did too."

Startled, Mary looked up to see if her mother was there – but of course she was not! She was in the hospital, miles away. Mary longed to be with her mother, to see her, to touch her. For months now, she had been playing the role of mother to her kid brothers and sisters – now, suddenly, she wanted her mother to hold her and comfort her.

"Forgive him," repeated the mother's voice. "If you can't do it on your own, ask for God's help to forgive him,"

Mary closed her tear-filled eyes. "Please God," she prayed. "Don't let my heart harden to stone. Help me to understand. Help me to forgive!" She remembered the slim man's anguished face and trembling voice saying, "I'm sorry! I'm so sorry!"

She had heard from her father that he had been calling the hospital constantly to enquire after her mother. He too had suffered because of the accident. He had a wife and small children, and he had lost his job after the crash. He had been talking to both her father and the hospital, and had even come to visit her mother once. He did care – and he was sorry.

As Mary prayed that night, she found that her bitterness began to dissolve. The hatred in her heart vanished, and she felt compassion for the first time. She thought of the guilt and the heartache the driver must have suffered, and her heart went out to his family.

Suddenly, the phone rang.

It was 12:30 a.m. Mary lifted the receiver with trembling hands.

"Honey, it's Mom," she heard as if in a dream. "The switchboard is closed for the night, so I came over to the payphone to talk to you. How are you my darling?"

"But ... but Mom, how did you get to the phone at this time of night?" Mary stammered.

She had heard from her Dad that her mother still suffered from severe dizziness, which prevented her from walking upright. Whenever she had tried to get up from her bed and walk on her own, she had fallen down and lay helplessly on the floor, until someone came to her aid. How could she have come up to the payphone? May be someone helped her.

"Mary, are you all right?" she repeated.

"I am fine Mom," Mary blurted out, a smile spreading across her tear stained face. "I'm just fine. Tell me, how are you?"

"At peace," came the mother's reply.

"So am I Mom," Mary whispered. "So am I. Finally, I have forgiven him. I just spoke to God before you called, and I feel a burden has been lifted from my heart. I have forgiven the driver who caused your accident."

"Mr. Abbott will be so relieved," said her mother. "Your Dad and I have forgiven him long ago. But he still remembers what you said, and he has asked me again and again if you would ever forgive him. He was here to see me today, you know."

Mary felt a lump in her throat. "Next time he calls, Mom," she said, "tell him please."

Six weeks later, Mary's mother came back home, almost completely recovered. The accident taught Mary valuable lessons – she learnt to forgive and be forgiven. She says she still hears her mother's voice, "Ask God to help you forgive him." It made a great difference in her life!

Forgiveness is not just a favour you confer upon another person. It is a much-needed protection you need for yourself. It protects you from corrosive feelings of bitterness and anger that can corrupt mind and soul. There are four simple principles we have to follow, in order to forgive in the best spirit:

- Stop being judgemental. We do not have all the facts necessary to make a fair judgement – so the best thing is to leave it to God.
- Develop the spirit of tolerance and understanding. Human beings are not perfect and we are all bound to make mistakes.
- Control the animalistic impulse to fight, hit back and hurt.

- Pray constantly for God's help. Sometimes, forgiveness is so difficult that we cannot do it alone. It requires the grace of God to change our minds and change ourselves. God's grace can dissolve even the most deep seated bitterness.

I read about a cancer specialist in New York, who was highly regarded in his field. He begins his treatment of every new patient with two special sessions. The first is called the Hour of Forgiveness. The second is called the Hour of Love.

This doctor believes that emotional factors have a leading role to play in causing and healing cancer, and therefore he summons all the patient's close family members for these sessions. In the first session – the Hour of Forgiveness – each person is asked to talk openly about the hurt or grievance caused by the patient. When these have been brought out in the open, they are asked to forgive the patient freely and openly.

In the second session – the Hour of Love – everyone involved expresses their love and goodwill for everyone else – especially the patient. The doctor is convinced that this beautiful sequence – first forgiveness, then love – creates the right atmosphere in which healing forces can work efficiently!

Vijay was a young engineer who worked in a factory that was situated 40 kms. away from the city, in a backward rural district of Maharashtra. One evening, as he was driving back home to the city, his car hit a young woman who ran across the road all of a sudden. Though Vijay braked, he could not stop the vehicle. The young woman fell on the road, in a pool of blood. Getting down from the car, Vijay saw with horror that she was pregnant!

What followed was a nightmare. Villagers helped Vijay to rush the woman to the nearest hospital. The police were informed, and registered a case against him and allowed him to go home. The woman's husband, a peasant, had been told of the tragedy in the meanwhile. Even as Vijay tried to explain how it had all happened, the young woman breathed her last. She had lost too much blood, and had suffered severe internal injuries.

A few weeks later, Vijay was summoned to appear in the local magistrate's court where charges were to be filed against him.

To his surprise, the woman's husband did not press charges against him. He had heard from the villagers that his wife had crossed the road rashly, ignoring the oncoming car. "The young *sahib* is not to blame," he told the judge quietly. "He should not be made to suffer for what is not his fault."

Vijay was free. He was let off – without even a fine.

Forgiveness sets us free. It gives us the opportunity to start afresh, to do better next time. It allows us to be freed from the grievances, penalties, and shackles of past mistakes. It heals the one who forgives – and the one who is forgiven.

Within us there is a conflict between love and hate. Love asks to forgive, hatred seeks to get even, to return evil for evil.

– J. P. Vaswani

The weak can never forgive. Forgiveness is the attribute of the strong.

Mahatma Gandhi

Keep on forgiving until it hurts!
Atleast forgive as many times as you would wish to be forgiven by God.

– J. P. Vaswani

Bury The Past

It was Ralph Waldo Emerson who said:

Be not a slave of your own past – plunge into the sublime seas, dive deep and swim far, so you shall come back with self-respect, with new power, with an advanced experience that shall explain and overtake the old.

We must learn to live in the present. We must attend to our present needs, resolve our present problems. We can hope and pray and plan for the future – but we must learn to leave the past alone. This is why Jesus said, "Let the dead bury the dead." To dwell in the past, to obsess about the past, to refuse to let bygones be bygones is akin to death.

Have you heard of Burke and Hare? Chances are that many of you have not! They were notorious rather than famous. They were two crooks who realised that they could make a fortune by digging up fresh graves, stealing the dead bodies buried therein and selling them to medical schools which needed corpses for their anatomy classes. (This was in the 1820s.)

"Ugh!" you are likely to say. "What a dreadful thing to do!"

You are right, of course. It is terrible to contemplate. But are we any better? Can I suggest to you that many of us are grave robbers without actually being aware of it?

Let me say to you, every time you dig up an old grievance, every time you relive the wrongs that you suffered in the past, every time you revive an old animosity – either by thinking about it or talking about it – you too are digging up an old grave. And you know very well what you are likely to find in it ...

Life is too precious to be spent in such pursuits. The past is over and done with. It is gone with the wind! Therefore, I say to you, release it once and for all! Let it go! This is the best way to handle all your failures, disappointments, hurdles, and grievances – release them, let them go!

We can do this simply by erasing the slate of our mind. We can refuse to think of them – and just deny their existence in our mind.

You see, the only existence they have is in your mind!

The present is beautiful, valuable, full of life, wonder and interest. It offers a glorious prospect for all of us. How foolish of us then to waste our energy and spirit in clinging on to the dead past! Therefore, leave the past! Set it free! Why should we demean ourselves, devalue our life digging out graves, poking and prodding dead bones of past mistakes and failures? Let the past be in the past.

Repeat to yourself the words – I am made for this day. It is the happiest day of my life – it can be the most successful day, if God so wills!

To live fully in the present, we have to be free from the burden of the past. If we do not heal past wounds and let the past go, we will be trapped in the past. And when we are trapped in the past, we cannot enjoy the present.

The past is like old, uncleansed residue that needs to be wiped out and released. For many of us long-forgotten sorrows, anguish and pain, frustrated ambitions and thwarted dreams lie locked up and stored in the dark, deep recesses of our memory. We must be courageous, seek God's help and release these dark forces. As Alan Cohen says, "The road to healing begins not with a blind leap outward, but by a gentle step inward."

Let us, by all means, learn from our past mistakes. This is a constructive, creative way of dealing with the past. But holding on to the guilt, shame and anger of the past is defeatist and destructive.

"I saw that all things I feared, and which feared me, have nothing good or bad in them, save insofar as the mind was affected by them," wrote the philosopher Spinoza. When you heal the past, your life will surely take on new meaning.

There was a woman who had led a life of immorality and crime. Her past was indeed unsavoury but she had resolutely turned over a new leaf, and was bravely attempting to walk the straight and narrow path.

But the authorities continued to trouble her, often suspecting her of committing crimes which had nothing to do with her.

"How can I get away from my yesterdays if you shove my past into my today?" she lamented. "I have tried to let the dead past bury the dead. But the State of California wants to make my past my present!"

God deals very differently, even with persistent sinners who seek His mercy and His forgiveness. Does He not say to us in the *Gita*: "Renouncing all rites and rituals come to Me for single refuge. Grieve not, for I shall release you from all bondage to sin and suffering."

A similar promise is given to us in the Old Testament – "For I will be merciful to their unrighteousness, and their sins and iniquities will I remember no more."

A young woman was censured by her priest, for not coming to the confessional for a long time. When finally she came, he told her sternly to confess her sins of yesterday, last week, last month, and last year. She replied, "I have none!" The priest reprimanded her, "You are either a great saint or an awful liar!" Perhaps the woman had confessed her sins to God and found full forgiveness!

Have you ever tried to talk to embittered people? They dwell insistently on the wrongs of the past. They cling on to the tiniest details of their bitter memories.

They smother themselves in self-pity. They take great pride and a gloomy satisfaction in listing and numbering every offence that was ever committed against them. They are ever ready to tell everyone how much they have suffered, how badly they have been hurt.

They nourish their hatred and resentment as if they were precious possessions. Alas, the very idea of forgiveness does not appeal to them – they feel that they have been so hurt, so offended, so wounded, so deeply injured, that they are exempted from the need to forgive.

But it is just these people who need to practise forgiveness! They are virtually choking under their own pent up resentment and hatred, that they are doing themselves irreparable harm. Their hearts are so filled with ill-will and rancour that they lose their capacity to love.

Bitterness about the past is not merely negative – it is destructive and self-destructive.

Forgiveness saves the expense of anger, the cost of hatred, the waste of spirits.

Hannah Moore

Forget What God Has Forgotten

To err is human, to forgive divine. The more you learn to forgive, the more Godlike you become. God is the Ever-free. The 'f' of forgiveness is freedom. Forgiveness sets us free from the hurts which otherwise would continue to prick us for as long as our memory lasts.

Within us there is the conflict between love and hate. Love asks to forgive, hatred seeks to get even, to return evil for evil. Has someone hurt me, cheated me, betrayed my trust, exploited me, spread scandals against me? Love tells me to forgive, hatred cries to get even, to take an eye for an eye, to give a blow for a blow. In the struggle, if love triumphs, I easily forgive the wrong doer. If hatred has the upper hand, the memory of wrong done to me keeps on burning within me.

Several years ago, a man met me. His face was dark as charcoal. He said to me, "There is a fire burning within me, and its flames will not be quenched until I have shot down the man who was indirectly responsible for the death of my father!" Yes – hatred is a fire that keeps on burning within you. It burns away your peace and happiness.

On the other hand, think of Mahatma Gandhi. He was nearly slain by a fanatic in 1908, when he was in South Africa. Mahatma Gandhi said to his friends, "This man did not know what he was doing. I will love him and win his love!" A year later, the man who wished to kill him, wrote to Mahatma Gandhi, offering his apologies and admiration. This is the magic of forgiveness.

There is a similar incident in the life of Pope John Paul II. A man named Muhamad Ali tried to kill him in 1984. The Pope went to the Rabibbia Prison in Rome to meet the man. The Pope took the hand of the man who had fired a bullet at his heart, and forgave him.

Sadhu Vaswani's repeated teaching was, "To live is to love". Our hearts must be so full of love that there can be no room in them for hatred to anyone.

When China invaded India, there were many in this country who hated the Chinese. Even in those

73

dark days, Sadhu Vaswani was concerned for their welfare as human beings.

When he was asked, "Don't you regard anyone as your enemy?" he answered, "In my heart is limitless love for the Lord. And I find there is not an empty corner in my heart for enmity to anyone. By God's grace, there is not one whom I may regard as my enemy."

There was a man who led an evil life. He drank and gambled, and he ill-treated his wife. His wife and children sought comfort at Sadhu Vaswani's *satsang*. He did not approve of this.

One day, the man came to Sadhu Vaswani and shook his fist at him and said, "If only you knew how much I hate you!"

Sadhu Vaswani looked lovingly at the man and said to him, "If only you knew how much I love you!"

What was there in Sadhu Vaswani's words? The man came and fell at his feet and, with tears in his eyes, begged forgiveness. His life was changed. He turned away from his evil ways. He accompanied his wife and children every evening to the *satsang*.

Forgiveness has the power to transform people!

Sadhu Vaswani, Mahatma Gandhi and the Pope were great men committed to the ideal of forgiveness. Let me give you an incident which occurred in the life of an ordinary man. He found a boy thief in his flower garden. Quietly, he came up behind him, caught the boy by his shoulder and said to him, "My boy, tell me which is the best flower in the garden?"

The boy, finding it impossible to escape, looked around and said, "That rose is the best."

The man, still holding the boy by his shoulder, plucked the rose in all its beauty and handed it over to the boy.

Amazed, the boy asked, "Aren't you going to punish me?"

"No," said the man. "I am not going to punish you. But I am going to trust you that you will never steal from my flower-beds again, will you?"

"Never, Sir, as long as I live," was the emphatic reply. "But please, Sir, tell me if there is any little thing that I can do for you. I would wish to serve you as long as I live!"

There is the magic of forgiveness. Forgiveness and a token of love had won the hardened heart of the boy and he became a willing servant of the rich man!

Learn To Let Go...

Betrayal, hurt, anger, disappointment – sometime or the other, we have to face these negative emotions in our life. When we dwell on other people's rudeness and insensitivity, we walk into the trap of bitterness and negativism. You constantly think about your disappointment; and then you begin to talk about it and you are trapped in resentment.

How best can we face such disappointments and frustrations? You can *choose* to react differently, by taking responsibility for your own emotions and feelings. You do this in the full awareness that others do not 'cause' your feelings. You *choose* your own.

It may be a cliché to say that it is useless to cry over spilt milk. But it's only too true. We have to learn to let go of disappointments and get on with our life. We need to forgive.

This is especially difficult when other people don't seek our forgiveness, or indeed when they are clearly in the wrong and don't deserve to be forgiven.

Never mind – let go!

In such situations, forgiveness allows you to let go of a no-win situation and walk out of it unhurt, unscarred by bitterness.

People alas, are not perfect. At home, at work, people are going to hurt you or let you down at one time or another. If we remained in charge of our feelings, if we are in control of ourselves, we can be two steps ahead of the situation. We will not be victims of circumstances.

Let me give you a small exercise. Think of two people who have hurt you, made you angry or let you down recently – two people about whom you still feel animosity.

Now ask yourself: what is my animosity doing to me? Do I feel happy holding on to it? Does it make me feel happier? Does it improve my sleep? Is my life better, richer, more meaningful because of my resentment?

If the answer to all the above questions is NO – then take a courageous decision.

Let go! Walk away from the disappointment and the bitterness!

We are most like beasts when we kill.

We are most like men when we judge.

We are most like God when we forgive.

Anon.

The 'f' of forgiveness is freedom. Forgiveness sets us free from the hurts, which otherwise would continue to prick us, for as long as memory lasts.

J. P. Vaswani

Four Stages Of Forgiveness

To arrive at forgiveness, one has to pass through four stages.

The first is the stage of hurt. Someone has wronged me, done something mean to me. Someone has been unfair to me and I cannot forget it. I feel hurt. The hurt keeps on throbbing within me. It is here that we must remember that it is not I who feels hurt, but the ego.

A woman met a holy man and confessed that she had resentment in her heart against a prominent sister of the community.

The holy man said to her, "Go to her immediately. Don't try to justify or excuse yourself. Tell her that you have had unkind thoughts about her. Be humble and ask for forgiveness."

The woman said, "I can't do that. I can't forget the hurt she had inflicted on me."

The woman was at the first stage – the stage of hurt. Those that are at this stage naturally hold grudges, not realising that the person who holds a grudge injures himself more than the one against whom the grudge is held.

Hatred and malice, like anger and worry, bring harm to the body, since they poison the blood. And they keep on increasing, for "a grudge is the only thing that does not get better when it is nursed."

Hurt leads to hate, which is the second stage. I cannot forget how much I have been hurt and I cannot send out thoughts of goodwill to my enemy. In some cases, I hate the person so much that I want him or her to suffer, as much as I am suffering.

Madam Chiang Kai Shek, we read, hated the Japanese. Her mother was a pious woman who prayed often. Madam Chiang Kai Shek said to her, "Why don't you pray to God that He may drown Japan in the waters of the ocean?"

Her mother, of course, said to her, "My child, how can I offer such an evil prayer?"

Hatred was painted by an artist as an old man shrivelled up and pale as death, clutching in his claws lighted torches and serpents, and cruelly tearing out his own heart with black, decayed teeth.

Asked to explain the significance of the picture, the artist said, "Hatred is an old man because it is as ancient as mankind, pale because he who hates, torments himself and lives a tragic life, with claws because it is so unmerciful, with torches and serpents because it creates discord, and it tears out its heart because it is self-destructive."

Hurt leads to hate. Then comes the third stage of healing. God's grace descends on me and I begin to see the person who has hurt me in a new light. I begin to understand his or her difficulty. My memory is healed and I am free again.

A girl came to a holy man and said, "I know not why, but I am unable to sit in silence and pray or meditate. I feel restless. I used to be so happy."

The holy man asked, "How is it?"

The girl answered, "I think it has something to do with one whom, at one time, I regarded as a friend. But she was very cruel to me, and I said that I would never forgive her, never talk to her. I am sorry I said it, but since then there has been no peace in my heart. What shall I do?"

The holy man said, "It is better to break a bad vow than to keep it. Go to her and seek her forgiveness."

The next morning, she went to her friend and confessed her uncharitable attitude and asked her forgiveness.

The one whose forgiveness was sought burst into tears.

She said, "You have come to ask for forgiveness. It is I who should be asking for forgiveness, for I am ashamed of my wrong attitude."

The two friends were reconciled.

Then comes the fourth stage of coming together. I am anxious to make friends with the person who hurt me, I invite him into my life. I share my love with him and we both move to a new and healed relationship.

We win by tenderness; we conquer by forgiveness.

Frederick W. Robertson

Apologising With Grace

When we are in a position of having to seek others' forgiveness, it is essential to apologise with grace. As Edward Kennedy puts it, "It takes two sides to make a lasting peace, but it only takes one to take the first step." The Senator was talking about reconciliation between nations. When we talk of establishing a relationship of peace with others, we can take the first step by saying, "I'm sorry!"

When we have erred, and caused grief and pain to others, anger builds up in the other person, while we ourselves carry a feeling of guilt. Many people tend to pass the blame on to others. We always try to fend off guilt. We try to escape from the situation, or we destroy worthwhile relationships.

It was Confucius who said, "A man who has committed a mistake and doesn't correct it, is committing another mistake."

We must accept responsibility for our errors and wrong doings. As Cardinal De Retz puts it, "The man who can own up to his error is greater than he who merely knows how to avoid making it."

People find it difficult to apologise for two reasons. First of all, their ego equates apology with losing or defeat of some sort. Secondly, it takes courage to apologise, and many people, sadly, lack courage. When I say 'apologise' I do not mean the lip service of mumbling 'I'm sorry', without meaning it. I mean expressing true and sincere repentance for causing grief and pain to another.

Apology is not defeat. Indeed it is a sense of victory over the self and over a bad situation which ceases to be irreparable once you apologise. Apology is also a spiritual triumph because it reduces tension, guilt, anger, and suffering on all sides. If only we care to admit it, the guilt that we suffer and the anger of the other person are really the result of our unwillingness to apologise.

Apology is not humiliation. It shows that we are mature enough to take responsibility for our actions. It also shows that we care about others' feelings and value our relationship with them.

Here are a few tips that I read on giving and receiving an apology.

- Do not mumble indistinctly. Do not turn your eyes away when you apologise. Look the person directly in the eye, and speak clearly and calmly.

- Do not shift the blame on to others. Assume responsibility for your actions and say, "It was my fault, and I am sincerely sorry."

- Look at the incident from the other person's point of view. Try to understand his feelings. Tell him or her, "I understand how you feel."

- Try to explain how the mistake occurred.

- Discuss a way out of the problem you have caused.

- You may follow the apology with a gift or a token of your genuine feelings. If you have caused the loss of an object, you must offer to replace it.

- When it is your turn to receive an apology look the person in the eye. Listen carefully to what he is saying.

- Do not dismiss an apology with a curt, "That's ok," or "Forget it," or "Doesn't matter." This creates the impression that you don't really mean it.

- Be gracious enough to thank the other person and appreciate his apology.

- Accept the apology with genuineness and sincerity. Respond with positive feelings and put aside all anger and resentment.

- Do not begin to list all the ways in which the other person has offended you. Do not get 'historical' – by bringing out all your past grievances against him.

- Do not ever remind him of what he did.

- Do not make excessive demands upon the person.

- Tell him how much better you feel after his apology.

- Give your best to building up the relationship after the apology.

When an apology is given and taken in the right spirit, it can build strong bonds and increase mutual respect.

Restoring Relationships

Any relationship between couples, parents and children, siblings, friends or colleagues involves two people, two human beings, neither of whom is perfect. To err is human, as we all know. We have our sins of omission and commission, through which we hurt each other. Just think of all the actions that strain a relationship – lying, cheating, indifference, apathy, shirking our responsibility, shifting the blame on to the other person, use of abusive language, violence and betrayal. Alas, the bitter truth is that all this happens, not between strangers, but between two people who are very close to each other. Such acts cause emotional injuries which do not heal easily. And relationships are jeopardised.

We need to practise the art of forgiveness if we wish to restore our relationships. No emotional hurt can be unforgivable. With a little effort, we can put them behind us to effect a reconciliation with our loved ones and friends, thus restoring peace within our minds and hearts.

Forgiveness, as in contrast to retaliation, is not an instinctive or spontaneous impulse. If we are hurt, almost as a reflex, we are conditioned to think, "I'll fight back – I'll do to you what you did to me." On the other hand, forgiveness has to be cultivated. It is a well-considered, well-thought out emotional choice that we make to forgive freely, those who have hurt us. For as we all realise, forgiveness does not just consist of mouthing the words, "I forgive you." It involves letting go of anger, resentment, hurt and bitterness. It allows us to heal the other – and be healed ourselves in the process.

Happily for most of us, we will never have to face the situation of forgiving a rapist or a murderer. However, every day we face the need to forgive a spouse, a parent, a child, a colleague, a friend, a neighbour, or even a perfect stranger. This is no easy task either.

People find it is easier to forgive a stranger or an acquaintance than to forgive a friend or relative, someone whom we know and trust. At such times, we can only tell ourselves that in the end, we are not responsible for what others do to us – only for what we do to them.

There is another important fact that we often overlook in emotional disputes with those who are close to us. Rarely is a dispute one-sided. Somewhere, somehow, we have a share in what we regard as an offence against ourselves. However, in our grief and hurt, we become blind to our own faults, while we magnify the faults of others. A little reflection, a period of calm introspection and a little humility will set the balance right.

As C. S. Lewis says, "To love at all is to be vulnerable. The only place outside Heaven where you can be perfectly safe from all the dangers and perturbations of love is Hell."

Mother Teresa once said:

People ask me what advice I have for a married couple struggling in their relationship. I always answer: pray and forgive. And to young people from violent homes, I say: pray and forgive. And, even to the single mother with no family support: pray and forgive.

A happy and successful marriage is a continuous exercise in forgiveness, patience, tolerance and mutual understanding. Unless a husband and wife learn to forgive and forget constantly, their marriage will become a series of recriminations. It requires humility and courageous acknowledgement of our own failings, to apologise to a spouse. And yet this is what makes a marriage happy. I always say to married people of my acquaintance, "Don't let the sun set on your quarrel. And if you should quarrel late at night, don't let the sun rise on your quarrel." Yes, a loving husband and wife have to forgive each other almost daily!

We forgive to the extent that we love.

La Rochefoucauld

Putting Forgiveness Into Practice

1. *Forget the past.* Someone has said, "More difficult than forgiving others is to forgive oneself." As we forgive others, let us learn to forgive ourselves. God is the ever-forgiving one and forgives us whenever we go to Him with repentance in our hearts. We need to forgive ourselves. Therefore, let us learn from our mistakes and drop, once and for all, the burden of our errors and sins. Do not carry the heavy load of guilt, resentment and anger into the future. Eventually, the load will break you spiritually and emotionally. Learn your lessons from the mistakes of the past – and forget the mistakes themselves.

2. *Empty your mind of all negative emotions.* Get rid of fear, hatred, envy, and bitterness systematically, when you sit down in silence and reflection.

3. *Let goodwill flow out of you towards everything and everyone.*

4. *It takes guts to forgive.* Cultivate the determination and strength of mind required for forgiveness, so that you can forgive without strain.

5. *Be aware of your own mistakes.* When we consider our own weaknesses, it is easier for us to understand others' shortcomings.

6. *Develop positive thoughts about the other person.* Speak kindly about him.

7. *It helps to write a letter or a note of goodwill to the other person.* This reinforces your positive feelings, puts them on record, as it were.

8. *Forgive in the Name of the Lord.* Forgive others even as He forgives us all for our many failings. Draw your strength and courage from Him, who is the source of all mercy.

I think if God forgives us we must forgive ourselves. Otherwise it is almost like setting up ourselves as a higher tribunal than Him.

C.S. Lewis

Witness Of The Great Ones

We are under the influence of the unforgiving ego. It clamours an eye for an eye, a tooth for a tooth. The ego does not want to forgive. In the measure in which we are released from the tentacles of ego, in that measure we grow in the quality of forgiveness.

Forgiveness has been an essential element in the lives of all the great ones of humanity. Think of Jesus. He harmed no one, he hurt no one. Yet, they captured him, at night, and held a mock trial and sentenced him to be crucified. From the Cross, Jesus looked at his captors and prayed, "Father, forgive them, for they know not what they do!"

Sant Eknath was a picture of patience. He was always calm, unruffled, serene. Some of the wealthy people in the town were jealous of him. They hired a man and promised to reward him richly, if only he could make the saint lose his temper.

Every day, in the dark of the dawn, the Saint took a dip in the waters of the river. One day, as he returned to his cottage, after his morning bath, the hireling spat in his face. Quietly, the saint went back to the river and had a second dip. Once again, as he was on his way home, the man spat at him. This unholy act was repeated for as many as 107 times. The saint's patience was not tired. He went to the river and, for the 108th time, had a dip in the sacred waters. This time the heart of the hireling was touched. As the saint wended his way homeward, the man fell at his feet and implored forgiveness, "Forgive me, O saint of God! I have greatly sinned!" The man explained that he had been bribed by some of the wealthy people to make the saint lose his temper. It was the temptation of the reward that had made him behave so nastily.

"Forgive you, for what?" exclaimed the saint. "Today has been a unique day in my life. I have had 108 dips in the sacred waters. For this, I feel grateful." The saint added, "If only you had told me of the reward, I would have pretended to be angry, so that you could have claimed your reward!"

Think of Guru Amardas! He succeeded Guru Angad. Guru Angad's son, Datu, was disappointed. He felt it was his right to occupy the *Guru-gadi* (the seat of the Master). Full of anger, he came to Guru Amardas and said, "Till yesterday, you were but a servant in our home. Today, you have occupied the *Guru-gadi*" So saying, he kicked the aged Guru.

The Guru looked at him with compassionate eyes and said, "I am an old man and my bones are hard. They must have hurt your foot. Forgive me."

Such is the witness of the holy ones, the saints of God, who have appeared in all climes and in all countries.

Think of Rishi Dayanand, the illustrious founder of the Arya Samaj. He was known for his fearlessness and frankness. He spoke the truth without fear or favour and, in the process, won the displeasure of many influential religious leaders. Some of them bribed his cook, Jagannath, to administer slow poison in his food.

Rishi Dayanand became seriously ill. The doctors realised that the great leader had been poisoned and there was no hope of recovery. When Rishi Dayanand learnt of it, he called Jagannath and, giving him some money, said, "Escape to Nepal. Flee, while there is time. If my disciples learn of what has happened, they will kill you!"

Every great man has borne witness to the noble ideal of forgiveness.

Think of St. Teresa, the little flower. She lived in a convent – a life of goodness and purity and service – and this aroused jealousy among some of the other sisters. Some took advantage of her goodness. This is indeed a common complaint. People say to me, "You speak of the spirit of forgiveness. But if we continue to forgive, people take undue advantage of us." Teresa did not mind. She went a step further. She rejoiced when some of the other inmates of the convent took advantage of her.

She went on being humiliated, laughed at, chaffed. Some misunderstood her innocence and characterised it as stupidity. She did not mind. She went her way: she called it the "little way". She realised that until she had become nothing, until she had completely emptied herself, she would not be acceptable to the Lord. She understood that the key – the only key – to the portal of 'Being' is 'not-to-be.'

She wished to keep her cell clean and tidy. In her absence, some threw dirt and dust in her cell and made it unclean. She accepted it as God's Will: and never did a word of complaint leave her lips.

She was fond of a pretty little jug. Someone took it away. The pretty jug was replaced by a heavy, cracked one. "So much the better," she said to herself, "I will be free from attachment to things."

One evening, she could not find her lamp and had to go without her reading. She sat in the dark and experienced the joy of having absolute nothing.

When she did anything for anybody, she hated to be noticed. She willingly accepted the blame that was due to others. She never tried to explain to her superior that someone else was the culprit. When she was wrongly blamed for having broken a vase, she kissed the ground and promised to be more careful. She went out of her way to do things for a sister who was rude to her. Teresa persevered with tireless patience until the cross-grained sister became a devoted and gentle friend.

She forgave the hurts she did not deserve and, in her heart, there was nothing but love for those who regarded themselves as her enemies, but whom she thought of as children of God. She walked the way of forgiveness and became a saint. Today, she shines as a radiant star in the firmament of the world's spiritual leaders.

Once, thieves entered the *ashram* of Sri Ramana Maharishi at night. They were under the impression that they would find lots of money and expensive objects in the *ashram*, for the Maharishi had several wealthy followers and devotees who constantly visited him. But, to their anger and dismay, they found practically nothing worth stealing.

Suddenly they entered an inner chamber, where they came upon the Maharishi in deep meditation. Rudely they accosted him, demanding that he tell them where the money and valuables were kept. Getting no response from him, the men began to attack him.

A few disciples who had been awakened by the commotion rushed into the Maharishi's room, and were appalled by the sight that met their eyes. As for the thieves, they took to their heels and fled from the *ashram* in no time.

Incensed by the injury inflicted on their beloved Guru, the disciples seized sticks and stones and whatever they could lay their hands on, and decided to pursue the miscreants.

"Do not go after them," said the Maharishi. "Pause and reflect for a minute. If your teeth bite your tongue, do you knock them off?"

The disciples learnt the profound spiritual lesson that all of us – all human beings – are linked in a cosmic chain of Being. Where then, is there room for anger and resentment when others are a part of us, and everyone is part of a great Cosmic Whole?

Hatred and jealousy, anger and bitterness, are aroused in us due to *karmic* influences. When we allow ourselves to be overcome by such hatred, we are linking ourselves to the *karmic* processes of those whom we regard as our 'enemies'. The best way to overcome this adverse process is to return love for hatred; charity for anger; compassion for cruelty.

Guru Ramdas was out asking for his daily *biksha* (alms). He came to the door of a cottage and called, "Please give me alms, mother!"

The woman of the house was busy mopping the floor of the hut. "Go away!" she called. "I'm busy and I have nothing to give you!"

"Please give me something – anything!" begged the saint.

The woman came out in a rage. "You shorn-headed, useless beggar!" she shouted. "Why do you harass honest, hard-working people every day?"

"You are right, mother," agreed the Guru, "but I beg you to give me alms."

The irate woman threw the dirty water and the mopping cloth at him and shouted, "Take that and be gone!"

"God bless you, dear mother!" said the saint, taking the bit of cloth. He went to the river and washed himself and went home. He had nothing to eat that day, and sat down in deep meditation.

When he came out of his *samadhi*, he realised it was evening. He prepared for the daily *aarati*, but found that there was no wick for the lamp. His eye fell on the piece of cloth that the woman had thrown at him, and he tore it up to make several wicks. When the *aarati* was over, he said to himself, "God is infinitely kind, and out of the dirty piece of cloth thrown at me, bright and lighted wicks could be made! May God bless that woman!"

Sadhu Vaswani always returned love for hate. "Why do you do so?" he was asked. Quietly, he answered, "Each man gives what he has. God has given me nothing but love!"

Sadhu Vaswani blessed those that blamed him. He prayed for those that persecuted him. He was free from the prickings of desire, free from passion and ill-will. He was the very picture of peace. To see him was to recall the immortal words of the *Gita*:

Forsaking all desires,

Abandoning all pride of possession,

Selfless and without egoism,

He moves onwards,

And enters into Peace!

It is the peace of God. The *Gita* calls it *Brahma-Nirvana*.

One of his associates had greatly wronged Sadhu Vaswani just because his niece was not appointed as the head of the Mira School. He wrote a number of falsehoods against Sadhu Vaswani and his organisation in the newspaper, purchased copies of the same and distributed them free among many of those who attended Sadhu Vaswani's *satsang*. Sadhu

Vaswani was silent. He spoke not a word in self-defence.

After a few years, the man realised the grievous fault he had committed. He came and fell at Sadhu Vaswani's feet and, weeping like a child, said, "You are a true saint of God! I am a sinner. I spread falsehoods against you. Not once did you utter a word against me. Pray forgive this repentant sinner and tell me what I may do to repent."

Sadhu Vaswani lifted him up and, folding him in a warm embrace, said, "Weep not, brother. If you would repent aright, forget all that you have done – and remember God!"

They brought to Sadhu Vaswani, one day, a girl who had gone astray. He looked at her. There were tears of repentance in her eyes. He wiped her tears with his handkerchief and said, "Forget what God hath forgotten! Go and live a new life!" The girl's life was transformed. She came to the *satsang* every evening and, before returning home, she would make it a point to meet Sadhu Vaswani and get his blessings. He always met her with the love of a mother for her child.

Referring to this girl, Sadhu Vaswani once said, "Sin is whirlwind. Love is gravitation!"

Speaking on sin and sinners, Sadhu Vaswani said, "David had committed many sins. Yet the Bible speaks of him as 'the man according to God's own heart!' In the heart of David was humility. And is there a greater sin than pride which is conscious of no sin?"

Sadhu Vaswani also said, "The sinner of today may be a saint tomorrow. Give him the pure love of your heart, and he will turn back!"

> If I do not forgive everyone, I shall be untrue to myself.
>
> *Albert Schweitzer*

Practical Suggestion No. 1
When anyone hurts you, immediately offer a prayer to God

The Lord's prayer exhorts us to forgive others, even as we expect God to forgive us.

Forgive us our trespasses, as we forgive those who trespass against us...

When we are in pain and anguish, we are 'out of sync', as they say, out of alignment with the source of all love and mercy. In such a state, our impulse is to hurt, hit out at the other person, inflict on him the pain that he has given to us. Thus, pain and hurt become a vicious cycle in our lives.

Such a negative situation can be overcome only through the healing power of God's love. And so, I urge my friends to turn to God with this prayer: "O God, help me to forget this hurt, so that it does not enter into my heart, and become a festering wound."

God's grace turns your negative, destructive emotions into love. While you cannot control another person's attitude to you or his emotions for you, you can choose your own attitude. You can choose what you want to experience.

When we strengthen our connection with God, we connect ourselves to His infinite mercy and compassion. Some of it will surely flow into our hearts, and we will be able to extend compassion, forgiveness and understanding to those who have wronged us.

It is natural for many of us to react with anger when someone has wronged us. We may even say, "How can I ever forgive what this person has done to me?"

My suggestion is to set yourself – your ego – aside and allow God's forgiveness to flow through you. Forgive for His sake. Let His forgiveness flow through you!

When you allow yourself to become the instrument of God's love and forgiveness, your inner life is transformed. Your heart softens and is cleansed of all the negative emotions you harboured earlier. There is a tremendous sense of release, as you are freed from the destructive effects of anger, hatred, resentment and bitterness.

You cannot obtain release from these destructive emotions on your own. It is God who can show you the way, teach you to forgive others even as He forgives you.

Here is what Susan Smith Jones tells us in her book, *Choose To Live Peacefully:*

> Forgiveness changes lives. Choosing to forgive unlocks the gate to healing and health, prosperity and abundance, joy and happiness and inner peace.

A Course In Miracles is a three-volume text on spiritual matters and peaceful living. The course shows how forgiveness can heal our minds, dispel our pain, and release us from the shackles of guilt and resentment. Forgiveness reunites us with God – and through forgiveness, miracles occur.

> God's answer is some form of peace. All pain
> is healed; all misery replaced with joy.
> All prison doors are opened. And all sin
> is understood as merely a mistake.

Charles Dickens, in his book *Tale of Two Cities,* writes about a man who had been imprisoned for

106

several long years, until he was almost forgotten! All those years he had longed for freedom from his dungeon. At long last, he was set free. They led him out of his dark cell into the bright and beautiful sunshine outside. For a moment he gazed at the blue sky and the bright sun – but his eyes were dazzled. He turned and walked back to his cell, covering his eyes with his hands. He had grown so used to the darkness, that he could not face the light anymore! The dark cell seemed to him to be a secure haven.

Like this man, we are chained by our negative emotions. We have become fixed, almost secure in these chains. We need to cast off the shackles – but freedom can come only to those of us who are willing to surrender ourselves to the Lord.

How true are the words of Jean Paul Richter – "Humanity is never so beautiful as when praying for forgiveness or else forgiving one another."

The Holy Qur'an tells us, "God does not change what is in people, until they change what is in themselves."

Therefore, it is up to us to take the first step. God will surely give us the courage to open our heart to the spirit of compassion and forgiveness.

The most difficult step on the road to forgiveness, healing and peace is the very first step. Once we take this step, with God's grace, we will find that His healing influence soothes our pain and affliction, washing away our grief and anger. God will give us the power to bury the past and unburden our souls of the accumulated bitterness and grievances of years!

Saint Vincent de Paul was a serving priest, but during a certain period of time, he had to interview job-seekers who were to be appointed for projects undertaken by the church. Once a mother came to him asking for her son to be employed. On examining the youth's credentials, the saint found him unsuitable, and told the mother so, politely.

The mother was so enraged that she picked up a heavy object and threw it at the priest's head, and stalked out of the room, slamming the door shut.

The saint calmly wiped the blood from his face, as his companion priest watched the scene in dumb-founded horror. Vincent de Paul remarked with a smile, "Isn't it amazing to see to what lengths a mother's love can go?"

That was a saint who spoke thus. But we can surely emulate him if we rise above the disappointments and annoyances of daily life and forgive those who offend us even before they ask forgiveness!

When forgiveness seems impossible, we must seek inspiration and strength from God – who is the ocean of forgiveness.

If you feel that an unforgiving attitude is festering in your heart, let me offer you a simple way out. It is a suggestion I make to everyone, in fact. Have a peace room or a peace corner in your home, to which you can go whenever you are disturbed by negative emotions. When someone has hurt you, and you find yourself unable to forgive and forget, retire to your peace corner and sit in quiet meditation for a while. Pour out your grief and pain to God and ask for His healing mercy to be poured upon your wounded heart and soul. If you do this sincerely, you will soon find yourself washed and bathed, as it were, in a shower of His grace and blessing. Allow yourself to be cleansed and purified in this shower of grace, and feel all your negative emotions being washed away. As you feel cleansed, breathe out a prayer for the person who has hurt you. Ask God to bless that person. Wish that person well. You will then find it easy to forgive and forget all the unpleasantness that threatened to overwhelm your life just a while ago!

Practical Suggestion No. 2
Unburden yourself to a Spiritual Elder

Sometimes, it is useful to write a letter to the person who has hurt you, the person against whom you hold a grudge. Unburden yourself in the letter. Pour into it all the venom that is within you. Write as many harsh words as you possibly can. After you have done so, tear the letter into pieces and, as you keep on tearing the letter, breathe out a prayer that God's benedictions may flow into the life of the wrong-doer.

A man came to Abraham Lincoln and complained that someone had acted horribly towards him and he could not forget the hurt.

Lincoln said, "Why don't you write to him a letter, telling him everything that you hold in your mind against him? Write as hard as you can."

The man went and wrote a very harsh letter, then came to Lincoln and said, "I have written the letter as you advised. May I now post it to him?"

"Of course not," said Lincoln. "Now you tear it up and throw the pieces into the fire and forget all about it!"

It becomes easier to forget when one has unburdened one's mind. This is why I recommend the technique of the letter that is not sent out.

However, if someone has hurt you to a point where you are unable to get over the hurt, unburden yourself to a spiritual elder. The same advice holds good when you are burdened by guilt, and wish to find a way out of your anguish.

A visiting pastor was preaching a sermon on "Love thy neighbour." He stressed upon the fact that a person who bore anger, ill-will and resentment in his heart, could not be a true Christian.

At the end of the sermon, the wife of the local priest met him with tears in her eyes. "I wish to be a true Christian," she said. "But I cannot overcome my resentment against Mrs. X, who is a prominent member of our Church."

The pastor said to her, "I advise you to go to her immediately. Do not try to justify yourself or make excuses for your attitude. Confess the truth to her. Tell her that you have harboured unkind thoughts about her. Be humble and ask her forgiveness."

"But I can't!" the woman trembled. "How could I ... What will she say?"

The pastor asked her to pray with him silently for a while. After a tearful prayer, she said submissively, "I shall go to her and apologise for Christ's sake."

The next morning she went to the lady and confessed her bitter feelings towards her, and begged her for forgiveness.

The lady burst into tears. "You are noble and loving," she said. "I am the one who should be apologising to you, for I too, have cherished un-Christian feelings towards you!"

The reconciliation of the two women whose animosity to each other was well-known, became the talking point of everyone in the Church. It set the standard, the example for everyone to emulate.

Priests, sages and spiritual elders often give us the right direction to follow as well as the spiritual courage we require to follow that path.

There were two merchants who were both disciples of the same Spiritual Master. Their shops were located just across the street from each other, and both were engaged in the same business, selling electrical accessories. They were friendly rivals when they started their business. A healthy spirit of competition prevailed between them. But in course of time, healthy competition turned to bitter rivalry and enmity. One thing led to another and they soon became irreconcilable enemies, often doing damage to each other's business.

There came a stage when one of them was overcome by remorse and shame at all that had happened. But how could he put back the clock? How could he make amends?

In a spirit of confusion and bewilderment, he unburdened himself to his Spiritual Master. "Guruji, I do not know a way out of this mess," he said. "It is you who must show me the right way!"

The Master said to him, "I have a simple solution. Do you think you will be able to put it into practice?"

"With your blessings, I can and I will," assured the merchant. "All I know is that I do not want to carry on with this intolerable situation. I want to make up with my competitor somehow or the other."

The Master told him, "Whenever a customer comes into your shop and asks for something you don't stock, direct him to your competitor's shop."

The man began to do so from the very next day. He would direct his customers to his rival's shop, if he couldn't supply what they wanted. It was not long before the rival realised what was happening. The enmity between them soon evaporated, and they were soon the best of friends!

A man came to his Guru and said, "My life is plunged in darkness. God seems to have deserted me. I have lost the great gift of happiness that I possessed sometime ago."

The Guru advised him to unburden his feelings. He came out with what was bothering him. His elder brother had betrayed him, cheated him over their father's will. Angry and upset, the man had sworn that he would never forgive him. Now, the brother was on his death-bed. He was all alone, for he had lost his wife and child. The man could not bring himself to go to him, for he had sworn never to forgive his brother.

The Guru listened to him with patience. In the end, he said, "My son, I urge you to go and offer your forgiveness to your brother."

The man went as he was bidden and a beautiful reconciliation was brought about. The brother died peacefully a few days later – and the man was freed from the terrible burden of resentment as he genuinely mourned the death of his brother.

I am often asked, "How can we overcome the fear of confessing to our Guru?"

I think I can suggest this. If I feel I cannot unburden myself to my Guru *in person*, let me take the picture of the Guru inside my room, and in the closed room, pour out my heart to the Guru. But I must be audible, I must actually express myself in words – not just silently within the heart.

We can also unburden ourselves before our *Ishta Deva*. We can bow before the picture of Sri Krishna, Christ, Guru Nanak, Buddha, Zoroaster or Baha'u'llah, or anyone else who to you is an image of Truth or God.

115

Just sit in front of the picture. Feel God's presence within you. Tell him, "I face this terrible situation! I have done this – or I feel resentment. I need *your* grace, I need *your* strength, *your* wisdom and *your* purity. Without it I am nowhere! I am helpless, and there are forces that drag me in the wrong direction. Please stand by me in this situation."

This will help you overcome your fear and your inhibition, and give you the courage to talk to the Guru and confess your weakness to him.

In fact there is one very good spiritual discipline that I suggest to all my friends. Every day, preferably at the same time, at the same place, sit in silence and think of all the things that you did in the last 24 hours. You will find that there are many things that you did which you should not have done, even as there are many things you did *not* do which you *should* have done. These are acts of omission and commission. Then ask for the strength not to repeat those mistakes. Repeat this exercise day after day as a *sadhana*, as a spiritual exercise. You will find that your life will change for the better!

In the outstanding novel *The Brothers Karamazov*, the great Russian novelist, Fyodor Dostoevsky writes

116

about a man who finally confesses to a murder that he had kept hidden for years. Having unburdened himself of his terrible guilt, he says, "I feel joy and peace for the first time after so many years. There is heaven in my heart...Now I dare to love my children and to kiss them."

What a tremendous sense of release and freedom we hear in those words!

Guilt thrives in dark places, in the secret recesses of the heart where the light of wisdom and understanding cannot penetrate. When it is brought out into the open, it is as if you have exorcised a ghost – it loses its hold over you. When we repress our guilt, we pile guilt upon guilt. When we unburden ourselves, accept responsibility for the wrongs we have done and own up to our guilt – we let the light into our lives, and free ourselves from self-torment.

The act of talking to a spiritual elder, paves the way for the liberating experience of forgiveness and reconciliation. If we deny ourselves this liberation, we will remain rooted in our guilt and pain.

Practical Suggestion No. 3
Learn to forgive yourself – do not carry the burden of guilt on your heart

Many of us carry on our hearts, heavy loads of guilt which rob us of our peace of mind. No man is perfect. Everyone of us has done some wrongs in the past, near or remote. We must repent and, if possible, make amends. We must pray for wisdom and strength not to repeat the wrong and then forget about it.

A husband told me that he and his wife had lived very happily for over fifteen years. Suddenly, something – he knew not what – happened and the wife – became aloof, sad and depressed. At times, he would find her sitting in a silent corner, shedding tears. This, he said, had spoilt the atmosphere of the house. He had talked to his wife, but there was no response.

I met the wife privately and understood that she carried a guilt feeling on her mind. I told her that

118

God is the great forgiver. He forgives: we must learn to accept his forgiveness and feel that we are forgiven. We must forgive ourselves!

She was a devotee of Sri Krishna. I said to her, "When you find that you are alone in the house, go and sit at the Lotus Feet of Lord Krishna and actually describe to Him all that had happened. It will not do merely to tell Him, 'Lord, You are the all-knowing One and already know whatever happened.' Actually recount, in detail, the things which you feel you should not have done, then ask for forgiveness – and then, what is very important, forget all about it."

"Will Sri Krishna forgive me all that I have done?" she asked.

I said to her, "Krishna forgives sins: by His power, sins are taken away and we can be free!"

That is the promise of Sri Krishna. Does He not say in the *Bhagavad Gita*, "Come unto Me for single refuge, and I shall liberate you from all bondage to sin and suffering. Of this have no doubt!"

She did as she was told. After some days, the couple met me again, and I rejoiced to find a radiant smile on the face of the wife. She said to me, "It is gone! It is gone!"

119

Many of us find it easy to forgive others but find it impossible to forgive ourselves. The Roman philosopher Cato, admits this when he says, "I can pardon everybody's mistakes except my own."

Yet learning to forgive oneself is one of the basic steps of cultivating the spirit of forgiveness for all. After all, if you cannot forgive yourself, how will you forgive others?

Forgiving oneself is essential for self-acceptance. This does not mean that we give up our moral or ethical standards and justify all our actions, both right and wrong. It only means that we learn to accept ourselves as we are, with our many shortcomings and a few merits.

For some reason people persist in being harsh and unforgiving with themselves. They become inflexible and judgemental. I know a man who carried a life-long sense of guilt because he could not become a doctor – something that his parents wanted him to do. Many mothers refuse to forgive themselves when their children do not turn out right. Wives blame themselves when a marriage breaks down...it is strange, but our acceptance of ourselves seems to depend on others' acceptance of us!

Self-criticism is healthy up to a point. But when it makes us ruthless, merciless jailors of our own conscience, it is time to let go of the guilt feelings and make a fresh attempt at self-knowledge, self-acceptance and cultivation of self-worth.

There is no end to the list of reasons for which people refuse to forgive themselves. These may originate from a person's culture, race, religion, gender or class. Many Catholics feel guilty about divorce. Puritans feel guilty about rest, relaxation and leisure. Many parents feel guilty about living on after they lose a child to death. Wealthy people suffer from guilt, because having more than others makes them uncomfortable. Alas, some poor people blame themselves for their poverty!

Our guilt may be due to personal standards that we have set for ourselves, as in the above cases. Or, they may be due to ethical reasons for having done something that is wrong. In either case, self-forgiveness is essential.

Self-forgiveness does not imply condoning wrong behaviour. Nor does it mean that you do not feel repentance for your past actions. Accepting this repentance, feeling remorse is part of the healing

121

process. But you must not let the remorse persist, as a permanent burden on your life. It is essential to overcome remorse, come to terms with your past and move on to face the future.

In Dostoevsky's famous novel *Crime And Punishment*, the hero commits the heinous crime of murder. At first, he refuses to acknowledge his guilt, but is tortured by fear and insecurity. This leads to such intense self-loathing, that he confesses his crime and accepts his sentence – fifteen years of penal servitude in Siberia. However, he is unable to forgive himself, until he accepts God's love and infinite mercy.

Persistent guilt feelings even lead some people to contemplate suicide. They feel they do not deserve to live. But this is the wrong way – the coward's way – out of the situation.

In the US, some courts give bold and innovative 'sentences' for criminals. They are made to do social work, or offer their services for the benefit of the underprivileged. Such a sentence has an extremely beneficial effect on their psyche, enabling them to grow in self-respect and self-worth. This is the starting point of acceptance and progress. It helps them escape from the conflict and turmoil that rages inside them and to learn to forgive themselves.

It was a wise man who remarked, "Unhappy is he who cannot forgive himself."

The moment that an individual accepts and forgives himself, is the moment of renewal, a new beginning.

> Stop judging others, and you will not be judged. Stop criticising others, or it will all come back on you. If you forgive others, you will be forgiven.
>
> *Jesus*

Practical Suggestion No. 4
Never hold resentment against anyone in the heart within. This can only harm you

If I hold a resentment against someone, I may not harm that person but will surely harm myself. Many suffer from bodily disease because of the grudges they hold in their minds against people.

A woman suffered from severe rheumatic pains in the knee joint. No medicines were of any avail. The pain went on increasing, until a holy man asked her, "Do you hold a grudge against anyone?"

She hesitated, then answered, "My mind is seething with resentment against my own sister who did not behave properly towards me."

The holy man said to her, "Your pains will disappear only when you forgive her and make peace with her."

At first, she found it difficult to do so. Later, she met her sister and gave her a hug and said to her, "Let bygones be bygones! Let us begin anew!"

To her amazement, she found that soon thereafter the pains disappeared.

A Course In Miracles teaches us that all disease arises out of our failure to forgive. Medical researchers are also of the opinion that an unforgiving nature may be one of the root causes of all human ailments. One researcher even calls arthritis "bottled hurt."

When we judge harshly, when we condemn or criticise, when we resent others or feel guilty about ourselves, we are hurting ourselves far more than we hurt others. Until we begin to practise forgiveness, we will be haunted by the bitterness of the past and the past will continue to repeat itself.

Emmet Fox observes:

> When you hold resentment against anyone, you are bound to that person by a cosmic link, a real tough mental chain.

You are tied by a cosmic tie to the thing you hate. The one person, perhaps in the whole world, whom you most dislike, is the very one to whom you are attaching yourself, by a hook that is stronger than steel.

125

Can you imagine what it is to be chained to another person by hate? The fetters of hatred bind both of you down. When you refuse to overcome your resentment and forgive the other person, you relinquish control over your life and emotions, connecting yourself to an explosive, negative, destructive power.

But once you free yourself from resentment and learn to forgive, you take control of your life and refuse to be controlled by the other person. Forgiveness is a change of heart. Forgiveness is a new lease of life. Forgiveness has the same effect on your tired mind and heart, as a week at a health spa has on your body.

Forgiveness is not a sign of weakness. It takes strength and courage and a generous spirit to understand that people do not wrong us or hurt us deliberately. Perhaps they could not help it, perhaps they need help, and their harmful actions and hurtful behaviour are nothing but cries for help!

Forgiveness brings profound peace into your life. It enhances the quality of your relationships, your career and your health. It restores the joy and harmony that was absent from your life while your resentment lasted. It is a great source of healing!

Raju and Ram were childhood friends. Their fathers and their fathers' fathers had been friends for generations. Their families owned adjacent pieces of land in the village, and the boys had gone to the same school, shared childhood pranks and grown up together.

As the years passed, the village was affected by a severe water shortage. Ground water levels had fallen so low, that reservoirs and wells had begun to run dry. There was just one common well where water was still available, and the farmers had to share the water.

An irrigation ditch was dug close to the well, and water was pumped into the ditch every day. Each farmer was allotted a turn at a specific time, when the water from the ditch would be diverted to his field. After the specified time, a dam would be put across his irrigation canal, and water would be diverted to another's field.

Under the stress and strain of sharing the water, the villagers began to squabble. Neighbours, friends and relatives exchanged heated words. Tempers flared and old bonds began to break with the strain.

Raju and Ramu met at the irrigation ditch one morning. Both needed water for their fields desperately. Each one wanted to have the water diverted immediately to his field.

A heated argument ensued. Both men were carrying shovels to open the canals that led to the fields. The shovels were wielded like weapons in the heat of the quarrel. Ramu's shovel hit one of Raju's eyes causing him to become permanently blind in that eye.

Raju could not forgive or forget the incident. Years passed, and anger and resentment grew in his heart until he was able to withstand it no longer. One evening, he took his hunting knife and walked out to the fields. Ramu was at the irrigation ditch, attending to his water-supply. Raju stabbed him to death with a single plunge of his knife.

The law took its course, and Raju was sentenced to life imprisonment for the pre-meditated cold-blooded murder of his childhood friend.

After ten years in prison, Raju became terminally ill. His wife sent a mercy petition to the State Governor asking clemency for her ailing husband. Ramu's grown-up sons opposed the move vehemently. They made it known all over the village that if Raju were released, they would kill him and his family members ...

This is how anger and an unforgiving nature shatters the peace of a whole community and destroys the lives of individuals and their families. The passion of a moment erupts into an irreparable action and results in life long resentment and vengeance that spans generations!

It is far better to forgive and forget than to hate and remember.

Anon.

Practical Suggestion No. 5
Make forgiveness a habit

We must not rest content by forgiving once or twice or thrice. We must keep on forgiving as often as we are wronged. God forgives us, again and again. Howsoever wayward or disobedient we become, He is never tired of forgiving us. He is patient until, at last, we return to Him.

A man met me in Indonesia. He spoke to me of one of his assistants who had reported against him six times to the tax authorities. Then, every time he came back and begged forgiveness. "I have reinstated him six times," he said. "How many times am I supposed to forgive such a man?"

I said to him, "A similar question was asked of Jesus. How many times shall we forgive? Shall we forgive seven times? And Jesus said, 'Seventy times seven!' Jesus meant to say that we must forgive as often as forgiveness is asked."

Forgiveness brings out the divine in us, as I said earlier. But we must be careful not to become egotistical or proud about our forgiving nature. There is no need for us to keep a reckoning – an event-by-event count of the number of times we have forgiven others and forgotten their offences. We should not flaunt our 'forgiveness score card' and feed our own vanity.

True forgiveness does not contribute to egoism and vanity. There is a beautiful saying about the violet, which spreads fragrance on the hand that crushes it. We too, must forgive silently, unostentatiously.

There was a poor elderly servant maid, whose task it was to make the royal beds on which the king and queen slept.

On a beautiful, full-moon night, the king and queen decided that they would sleep on the terrace of the royal palace, open to the sky. The old maid worked hard to lay the huge royal mattresses with their expensive and elaborate sheets and pillows. By the time the laborious task was finished, she was so exhausted that she sat down for a while to rest. The gentle breeze and the coolness of the moonlit night lulled her to sleep. Unaware of what she was doing, she lay on the royal bed and fell asleep.

You can imagine the wrath and ire of the royal couple when they discovered the humble, shabby figure of the old servant on their beautiful bed! The queen was beside herself with rage and ordered the royal attendant to lash her fifty times with a whip.

Trembling and humiliated, the servant bowed down low and felt the first furious whiplash on her back. She cried out in great agony. The second blow descended, and she screamed, yet again.

The third and the fourth followed in quick succession. She was silent. The sixth, seventh, eighth blow fell without even a movement from her. After the tenth, she started to laugh out aloud!

The attendant could not continue whipping any longer. He was stunned and amazed! How could she laugh in the face of such searing pain and humiliation?

The king and queen were also nonplussed by her behaviour. "Why are you laughing?" they demanded of her.

"You were not ready to forgive me my single offence," said the maid. "But I learnt to forgive you after the pain of the first two blows. But this thought amuses me, that for the pleasure of lying ten minutes upon a velvet mattress, I am condemned to be whipped fifty times. I thought of the fate of monarchs like you, who sleep on such beds every night of your life – I wondered how many lashes you would merit!"

The king realised the wisdom of her words and ordered the maid to be released immediately.

Many people ask me, "How can I forgive someone who goes on hurting me, time after time? At one time or another, I feel like retaliating. After all, it is said that one can expect an eye for an eye…"

Mahatma Gandhi once said, "An eye for an eye would leave the whole world half-blind." Hatred begets hatred. Vengeance begets vengeance. It is only the magic of forgiveness that can break the vicious cycle. The most intense hatred and bitterness can be conquered with the all-powerful healing force of forgiveness.

Man today, is a highly evolved creature. At this stage of human civilisation, how can we allow ourselves to revert to the primitive qualities of anger, violence, venom and vindictiveness? Modern weapons like guns and pistols and bombs can only destroy. Far more powerful are the spiritual weapons of non-violence, compassion and divine forgiveness!

All holy men advise us to make forgiveness more potent and more effective by practising it continually. Once is not enough! Forgive a hundred times! No effort is too great to destroy the evil within us – the evil passions of anger, bitterness, grudge, and resentment. How can we cease to practise forgiveness, until we have conquered ourselves?

The Duke of Orleans was appointed as the regent to the ruler of the realm when King Louis XV was very young. After several discussions and deliberations, it was decided that certain restrictions would be placed on the Duke, for he was only a regent, not a King.

The Duke examined carefully the clauses which restricted his powers. One of them, he refused to accept, outright. It was the clause which denied him the power of royal pardon.

He said to the Council of Ministers, "I have no objection to my hands being tied from doing harm. But I must have them free to do good!"

Practical Suggestion No. 6
Forgive before forgiveness is asked

It was Jesus who said, "Unto him that smiteth thee on one cheek, offer also the other!" He also said that if a man compelled you to walk with him for a mile, go with him an additional mile.

This teaching has great therapeutic value. Whosoever lives up to this teaching finds that his interior peace is never disturbed. And is not peace the solid foundation of health?

A quaker had a quarrelsome, disagreeable neighbour whose cow often got into the quaker's well-cultivated garden.

One morning, the quaker drove the cow to his neighbour's home and said to him, "Neighbour, I have driven thy cow home once more. If I find her in my garden yet again ..."

Before the quaker could finish the sentence, the neighbour said angrily, "Suppose you do? What will you do?"

"Why," said the quaker softly, "I'll drive her home to thee again!"

The cow didn't give the quaker any more trouble.

Many of us tend to regard forgiveness as an act of magnanimity and generosity when we are in a position to accept other's apologies and pardon their offences. But when the tables are turned and we have to beg someone's pardon, we find ourselves rather reluctant to do so with grace and humility and then, we regard it as our prerogative to obtain the other person's forgiveness as a matter of course.

The Lord's prayer, as I have said, enjoins us to forgive others as the Lord forgives us. In fact, we demand forgiveness of the Lord, on the implicit promise that we will forgive others who offend us. The example of the Lord is before us and therefore it behoves us to forgive others in the spirit of true love and understanding. This is not a matter of patting ourselves on the back, or taking credit for our merits.

"Judge not, that ye be not judged," said Jesus Christ. It is this non-judgemental attitude that is required in forgiving before forgiveness is asked.

Rabbi Leo Beck was a learned man, a German scholar who took on the painful task of leading the Jews in Germany during Hitler's regime. He was arrested five times and finally sent to a Concentration Camp.

Here too, he was elected to serve on the convicts' committee of management. Finally, like thousands of his brothers, he too was condemned to be shot!

On the day he was to be executed, Russian troops arrived at the Camp and the Jews were liberated. Beck could have escaped then and there, but he stayed behind to persuade the Russian soldiers to spare the lives of the German camp-guards who had terrorised the Jews till then.

In a quirky decision, the Russians handed over the guards to the inmates of the camp. Beck then argued with his fellow Jews and managed to persuade them not to take the vengeance that they were thirsting for. He was indeed an angel of compassion – and the Germans had not even begged his forgiveness or fallen at his feet!

The Duke of Wellington faced a painful task ahead of him. He had to pronounce the sentence of death on a confirmed deserter. It was a heart-rending situation for him, for he knew the man to be a brave and good soldier. With a heavy heart, he announced, "I am extremely sorry to pass this severe sentence, but we have tried everything, and all the disciplines and penalties have failed to improve this man."

Then the man's comrades were given an opportunity to speak for him.

"Please allow me to tell you, your Excellency," said one man, "that there is one thing you have not tried."

"Tell me what it is, my good man," said the Duke, taken aback by the man's comment.

"You have not tried forgiving him."

Willingly and spontaneously, the Duke granted his pardon to the soldier. And it worked, too! The soldier never again deserted, and remained grateful to the 'Iron Duke' ever after.

Clement Hofbauer was a dedicated servant of the Lord and his suffering children. He was a true saint who could not bear to see others suffer. For this man of God, Sadhu Vaswani's words could have been the motto of his life. Service of suffering humanity was worship of God.

Some people belittled his efforts and mocked his way of life. A scornful neighbour said to him, "Clement Hofbauer, your's is an idle and useless life. You neither earn yourself, nor do you allow others to earn their own living. Your so-called charity and service only encourages beggars and sponges. Give up this wasteful 'hobby' and turn to some useful occupation!"

The insults and humiliations heaped upon him did not detract Hofbauer from his chosen path. He carried on his noble task of service to the poor and the hungry.

Several years later, Hofbauer was on a tour, begging for aid to help his poor and neglected people. He literally had to beg people, appealing earnestly to one and all to give away whatever they could.

By chance, he came upon his erstwhile neighbour who had berated him so severely during those early days. Undaunted, the saint begged him to help the poor destitutes.

"You are shameless!" snarled the irate man, and spat on his face.

"Thank you," said the saint, quietly wiping his face. "That was for me! Now, perhaps, you might wish to give something for the poor?"

The man was stunned. His soul was shaken, and he fell at the saint's feet and begged his pardon. He followed this up with a big donation for the poor.

Hofbauer was a saint who forgave before forgiveness was asked.

When we refuse to let bitterness and resentment go, when we refuse to forgive, we remain bound by bitterness to those who have wronged us. This bitterness and resentment will poison our spirit, and contaminate our thoughts and attitudes. We will continue to remain wounded, hurt, and in pain... refusing to heal.

But when we let go of our anger and hatred, we realise that bitterness is nothing but wasted energy. Therefore, let us forgive even before forgiveness is asked. Let us forgive, even when no remorse is shown.

Alan Paton tells us, "There is a hard law... that when a deep injury is done to us, we can never recover until we forgive."

I wonder if you have heard of Fanny Crosby, the famous blind songwriter. She was just six years old when she developed a minor eye inflammation. The doctor who treated her was careless, and his wrong treatment caused her to become permanently blind.

Despite this tragic mishap, Fanny harboured no resentment against the physician. She forgave him and turned her blindness into a gift, rather than a handicap. In fact, she once remarked, "If I could meet that doctor now, I would thank him over and over for making me blind."

Fanny Crosby wrote more than 8000 songs. She felt that it was her blindness that helped her to write those beautiful hymns which flowed so prolifically from her pen. This extraordinarily gifted blind woman was convinced that God made her blind for a definite purpose, so that she could 'see' more clearly in other ways and lead men Godward with her inspiring music. People said of her that she allowed her tragedy to make her better and not bitter!

Langston Hughes was a black writer who lived and wrote his poetry during the 1920's and '30's when racial hatred and tension were at an all-time high in America. His poems are a tribute to the healing spirit of forgiveness. Here is a well-known poem of his:

I am the darker brother
They send me to eat in the kitchen
When company comes,
But I laugh,
And eat well,
And grow strong.
Tomorrow,
I'll sit at the table
When company comes.
Nobody dare
Say to me,
"Eat in the kitchen,"
Then.
Besides,
They'll see how beautiful I am
And be ashamed –
I, too, am America.

Here is a writer whose brothers and sisters were treated shamefully by white Americans. And yet we can see no resentment, no bitterness in his work. He laughs at himself and others. He asserts that he will grow strong and beautiful despite what people say about him. He rises far above narrow labels like black, white or brown. He reminds us of William Blake who wrote: "In Heaven, the only art of living, is forgetting and forgiving."

We can learn from the example of Hughes. No matter how foolish and prejudiced people may be, we have the choice to rise above their pettiness and forgive them freely – before they ask forgiveness.

There is a story told to us concerning the Buddha, and a man who wanted to test, perhaps trap him who was known as the Compassionate One. He had heard about the Buddha's principles of non-violence and peace. He wanted to put him and the principles to the test.

He travelled a long way to reach the Buddha's presence. Having got there, he began to abuse and insult the Buddha in every way he could. He chose the most insulting terms and the most insulting words. He blamed, criticised and found fault with everything that the Buddha said or did. And this went on for three days continuously.

Throughout this period, the Buddha did not falter or react negatively. To each rude comment, to each verbal attack made by the man, he responded with love, kindness and a beautiful smile.

The man could take it no longer. "Are you less than human or more than human?" he wondered aloud. "How could you swallow all those terrible insults and still not respond?"

In answer the Buddha had a question to ask: "If someone offered you a gift and you do not accept the gift, to whom does the gift belong?"

The man was answered. He had offered the gift of anger, hostility and insult to the Buddha. The master did not react in retaliation. Why should you be upset or angry about something which does not belong to you?

Mahatma Gandhi hated British rule in India – he had nothing against the British people themselves. Again and again, judges, civic administrators and even the governor-generals of the British regime had to punish him under strict laws but he treated them with courtesy and friendship, never ever harbouring personal animosity against anyone of them. We are told that a judge who was about to hear a serious complaint of sedition against Gandhiji, actually bowed to him before he took his seat.

Martin Luther King Jr. was inspired by Gandhiji's example. Here is what he had to say about the non-violent approach:

The non-violent approach does not immediately change the heart of the oppressor. It first does something to the hearts and souls of those committed to it. It gives them a new self-respect; it calls up resources of strength and courage that they did not know they had. Finally it reaches the opponent and so stirs his conscience that reconciliation becomes a reality.

In our own times, we have the splendid example of Nelson Mandela who was imprisoned by the racially oppressive apartheid regime in South Africa. When this regime could no longer sustain its power, Mandela was freed, and voted to power as the first black president of a free and equal nation. And yet he harboured no resentment or bitterness against his erstwhile oppressors – and the white people of South Africa suffered no reprisals or recriminations in his rule!

These great men really allowed themselves to become instruments of peace and healing, in a world troubled by hatred and violence!

Practical Suggestion No. 7
When you forgive – make sure you forget

Someone has said, I can forgive but I cannot forget. That is only another way of saying, I will not forgive. True forgiveness is like a cancelled cheque – torn and thrown into the waste paper basket.

There were two old friends who met each other, one evening, after several years. They decided to have dinner together. They sat and they talked, recalling many experiences of earlier days. Finally, one of them realised it was three o'clock in the morning. They said to each other, we must hurry home.

The next day, they met again and one said to the other, "How did your wife take your coming in so late, last night?"

The man replied, "I explained to her, she understood and it was perfectly alright. How did your wife react?"

146

The man answered, "When I got home, my wife became historical."

The friend said, "You mean hysterical?"

"No," said the man, "I mean historical. She brought up every wrong that I had done during the last thirty years of our married life!"

We must not be historical. When we forgive, we must forget. A friend of Clara Barton, founder of the American Red Cross, once reminded her of some cruel thing that had been done to her, years ago. But Miss Barton seemed not to recall it.

"Don't you remember it?" her friend asked.

"No," came the reply, "I distinctly remember forgetting that."

A man was on his death-bed. He held a grudge against a friend who had dealt with him unfairly. Before dying, he wanted to tell him that he had forgiven him. When the friend arrived, the man embraced him and said, "I am about to die. I forgive you for whatever has happened."

The friend felt relieved, and his eyes glistened with unbidden tears.

Before the friend left, the dying man said, "I forgive you only if I die. If I recover I take back my words."

Forgetfulness is very often a great lesson – though students who are struggling to remember their lessons at the time of an examination may not agree with me!

But I am not talking about that kind of forgetfulness. Many of us forget what we have to remember – we forget faces, names and people. Alas, we also forget to count our blessings, and all the good things that happen to us! This makes us ungrateful and ungracious.

However, there are some things which we never allow ourselves to forget. Unpleasant situations, bitter experiences, and people who have offended us knowingly or unknowingly. The Greek philosopher Themistocles says, "Teach me not the art of remembering, but the art of forgetting, for I remember some things that I do not wish to remember, but I cannot forget things I wish to forget."

We must learn to forget injuries, hurts, insults, and betrayals so that we may be healed – and those whom we resent and hate may also be healed in the process.

A noble French General, Lord Lamotte, was walking along a road in Lyons, when he was accosted by a drunken soldier who failed to recognise his superior officer.

In a rage, the General slapped the man on the face. But he instantly felt sorry for what he had done. The next day, he summoned the soldier and said to him, "Do you remember what I did to you yesterday?"

"Yes Sir," said the man impassively.

"I am afraid I remember it too! Can I offer you five francs?"

"I would not accept them, Sir – I'm sorry."

"Perhaps ten francs?"

"You cannot repay your slap with ten francs Sir," was the guarded reply.

"You are right," agreed the General. "So I'll tell you what – I'll embrace you and ..."

"Oh yes Sir! Let us embrace each other and forgive and forget!"

There was a man who had too much to drink at an office party. Like many people who lose control over themselves under the influence of alcohol, he began to make a foolish spectacle of himself -- singing loudly, passing silly remarks and finally ending up dancing with the lampshade as his hat, before he passed out.

He was brought home unconscious and put to bed by his wife. He awoke the next morning, ashamed and miserable. He begged his wife to forgive him, and she readily promised to do so.

Forgive she did – but forget she would not! As days went by, she would constantly remind him of the shameful incident which he so desperately wished to forget. In the end, the man was so humiliated that he said to her, "I thought you would forgive and forget what I did!"

"It *is* true that I have forgiven and forgotten," the wife assured him. "But I don't want you to forget that I have forgiven and forgotten."

When you forgive – learn to forget too! Forgiveness is not completed till you push out all thoughts of the past from your mind, until you free yourself from the impact of the wrong done to you, until you forget it all!

Practical Suggestion No. 8
Speak kindly concerning the person against whom you hold a grudge

It is not enough to speak kindly. In fact, you must go out of your way to help him, to serve him. That is the way God's grace will descend on you.

George Washington and Peter Miller were schoolmates. One became President of the U.S.A., the other, a Preacher. A man named Michael Wittman persecuted Peter Miller and troubled him in many ways.

Suddenly, Wittman was involved in a charge of treason and was sentenced to death.

Miller walked seventy miles to Philadelphia to see Washington, who asked, "Well, Peter, what can I do for you?"

"For the sake of our old acquaintance, George, I have come to beg the life of Wittman."

"No, Peter, ask for something else," said Washington. "This case is too black. I cannot give you the life of your friend."

"My friend!" exclaimed Miller. "He is the bitterest enemy any man ever had." And he described what he had suffered at the hands of Wittman for over twenty years.

As Washington heard the story of Peter's persecution, he said, "Ah, then, Peter, this puts another aspect upon the matter. You are pleading for the life not of a friend but your bitterest enemy. Surely, this is not the work of a man, it is something divine. I can refuse man, but I cannot refuse God. I will freely pardon your enemy."

An English officer walked through the battlefield with his servant. He noticed a wounded enemy soldier crying for water.

"Give the poor fellow a drink from my water-bottle," the officer said to the servant.

As the servant stooped down to give water to the thirsty soldier, he immediately fired at him.

"And now, Sir, what do I do?" asked the servant, stepping back.

The officer answered, "Give him the water, all the same!"

Amazed by Lincoln's constant attitude of courtesy and kindness towards his enemies, an elderly woman admonished him, "How can you speak kindly to them when it is your duty to destroy them?"

Lincoln smiled. "Madame, do I not destroy my enemies utterly and completely when I make them my friends?" he wanted to know.

Truly has it been said that there is no revenge so complete as forgiveness!

I always say there are no strangers, only friends and friends in the making. You can meet friends anywhere and everywhere but you can't meet enemies everywhere, because you have to *make* them. And it is better to forgive them and learn to love them because *you* made them! And when you love and forgive, you change an enemy into a friend!

A Chinese proverb says, "The greatest conqueror is he who overcomes his enemy without a blow."

When a friend makes a mistake, don't rub it in. Rub it out.

Anon.

153

Practical Suggestion No. 9
Rise above your resentment and actually love the person who has wronged you

There were two brothers who lived in adjacent farms separated by a creek. For years they lived together in peace and amity, sharing their implements and produce, exchanging labour and goods as they needed. Suddenly things turned sour between them. A small misunderstanding led to a major quarrel and they became sworn enemies.

The elder brother called a carpenter over to his farm. "Can you see the creek out there?" he asked. "Across the creek is my brother's farm. I want you to take all the lumber in my store house and build me a fence on this side of the creek so that I won't have to see his farm again!"

"I understand the situation," said the carpenter. "Just leave the job to me!"

154

The older brother had to go into town for some supplies and so he gave the carpenter all the material he needed, and departed for the day.

When he returned home, the carpenter was putting the finishing touches to his job. The farmer's jaw fell open at the sight that greeted his eyes.

There was no fence to be seen! Instead, there was a bridge, stretching across the creek, and linking the two farms as never before! What was more, the younger brother was walking across the bridge, with his arms outstretched, smiling.

"My dear brother, how splendid of you to build this bridge after all that I have said and done! I am so glad we are back on the same loving terms as before!"

The brothers met each other in a spirit of love and kindness. The carpenter watched with a smile as they embraced each other, and got ready to leave.

"Don't go yet," called the elder brother. "There is lots more you can do for us," said the younger brother.

"I must move on," said the carpenter. "I am sure there are many more bridges I have to build!"

When Abraham Lincoln was a young and struggling lawyer, he was thrilled to be employed as part of a legal team that was handling a very important lawsuit. The other lawyers on the team were experts and luminaries in the profession. When a leading lawyer among them, called Edwin Stanton, saw Lincoln, he remarked caustically, "Who is that gawky ape and what is he doing here? I refuse to work with him! Get rid of him!"

Lincoln remained calm, ignoring the insults heaped upon him. As the lawsuit got under way, he was ignored and ill-treated by the other lawyers. However, Lincoln followed the arguments in court carefully, as he wanted to learn all he could from the legal luminaries. He was especially thrilled by Stanton's masterful arguing of the case, his brilliant oratory, his expert preparations and his fluent presentation. "I can't hold a candle to his abilities," he remarked. "I am going home to study law all over again!"

Years later Lincoln rose to occupy the highest office in the land and Stanton continued to be his vocal critic. However, President Lincoln valued his brilliance, and when he needed a secretary of war his choice fell on Stanton, the very man who had insulted him all those years ago. By doing so , Lincoln revealed a sterling character that upheld a forgiving spirit rather than nurse a lifetime grudge.

It was no wonder then, that when Lincoln was shot by an assassin, Stanton was filled with grief and sorrow. He sobbed, heartbroken, even as he uttered the words, "Now he belongs to the ages!"

It was Laurence Sterne who remarked, "Only the brave know how to forgive... A coward never can...it is not in his nature."

An Arabic proverb advises us: "Write the wrongs that are done to you in sand, but write the good things that happen to you on a piece of marble. Let go of all emotions such as resentment and retaliation, which diminish you, and hold on to emotions such as gratitude and joy, which enhance you."

During the Korean War, the communists captured a man and ordered him to be shot for anti-party activities. Just before he was about to be executed, the communist leader was told that the man ran an orphanage that cared for several small children. The man's life had to be spared. But in an act of wanton cruelty, the party leader ordered that the man's son, a young boy, should be killed in his place.

Years passed. The war took a different turn, and the same communist leader was captured and condemned to death by his enemies. Now, the father whose son had been killed, pleaded for his life. "Let him live," pleaded the man. "I promise you I will make him turn over a new leaf."

The communist's life was spared. The father of the murdered boy not only forgave him, but took him home as his guest, treated him with love, cared for his wounds and showered him with kindness.

It was such a man who is described in the oft-quoted words of J. Harold Smith: "Never does a man stand so tall as when he forgoes revenge, and dares to forgive an injury."

Benjamin Disraeli, who became the Prime Minister of England in 1868, was another great soul, who extended kindness and courtesy to those who wronged him and insulted him.

Leech, a famous cartoonist who worked for the world-renowned weekly *Punch*, drew derogatory cartoons of Disraeli for about 30 years, continuously.

Yet, when he became PM, Disraeli helped Leech's family in many ways.

The famous essayist and historian, Thomas Carlyle, once branded Disraeli as an absurd, silly monkey and said, "How can you tolerate this fool dancing on your chest?"

During his second term as PM, Disraeli awarded Carlyle the highest honour as historian, forgetting all the abuse he had heaped upon him.

"How is it that you bear no grudge against such people?" a friend asked him. "How can you forget all that they have said and done against you?"

"It is just not in my nature," was all the great statesman would say!

It was this great man who once remarked, "We are all born for love... it is the principle of existence and its only end."

Rabia, the saint whom my Master Sadhu Vaswani, described as the 'Mira of Islam', was reading a holy book when she came across a sentence, *Abhor the wicked!*

Try as she might, she could not bring herself to accept this exhortation. In fact, it upset her so

159

much that she scraped it out of the book she was reading.

A few days later, a holy man of God visited her, staying as her guest for a couple of days. He asked for a book to read and was given the selfsame book where she had come across the sentence, *Abhor the wicked*.

When the saint saw the scraped sentence, he exclaimed, "Who has done this?"

"It was I," said Rabia. "I did it because it told me to abhor the wicked."

"But how could you tamper with a holy book?" exclaimed the holy man. "It is wilful and sinful!"

"That may be," said Rabia, courteous yet firm. "But I could not accept the dictum. Abhor someone! My very soul rebelled against the idea. How could I abhor anyone, howsoever wicked, when my heart overflows with love for all human beings? In fact, I do not know where I can harbour this feeling of abhorrence – for there is no place in my heart for such feelings!"

She was blessed with instinctive love for all humanity and the only thing she could hate was hatred itself!

160

Tarakant Roy was a high official at the King's court. One night, Roy returned home very late after an important meeting with the King. He was exhausted, and decided to go to bed immediately.

When he entered his bedroom, he saw that his valet was slumped on his bed, fast asleep.

Any other man would have been incensed at the sight of a servant sleeping on his bed but not Tarakant Roy, a loving and forgiving man. Quietly, he took a sheet from a cupboard, spread it on the floor and went to sleep.

Early the next morning, the King arrived at his house to discuss an urgent matter. He barged into his minister's room and stood dumbfounded at the sight of the servant sleeping soundly on the bed, while the master slept on the floor.

"How could you do this Roy saheb?" The King asked in amazement.

"I had no heart to disturb a tired man's sleep, your highness," Roy replied. "So I let him sleep on!"

There was a man who could forgive and love!

My beloved Master, Sadhu Vaswani, narrated to us a beautiful story of Hussain, the martyr of Karbala.

161

Once he was sitting at his dinner, and the slave was present to serve him. By an accident a hot dish fell on Hussain's knees.

The slave was terrified and recited a verse from the Holy Qur'an, "Paradise belongs to him who restrains his anger."

Hussain answered, "I am not angry."

The slave continued, "Paradise belongs to him who forgiveth his brother."

And Hussain said, "I forgive you!"

And the slave finished the verse, "For God loves the benevolent."

Immediately, Hussain responded, "I give you liberty! No longer are you my slave: and I give you four hundred pieces of silver!"

Truly, God loves men of compassion, God loves those who forgive their fellow men!

A little boy called Peter was playing with his friend on a sunny Saturday afternoon. They hit upon a mindless but dangerous game – throwing stones on to the roof of a nearby bungalow, to watch how they came sliding down the roof into the backyard. Peter picked up a smooth, round stone and aimed it at the roof. He missed completely and the stone shattered the kitchen window.

The boys fled from the scene in panic. But Peter could not be at peace with himself. He knew the old lady who lived alone in the bungalow. She was his customer on his paper-route. She was a kind and gentle soul, and he was contrite that he had caused damage to her house, although unwittingly. However, he did not have the courage to own up his mistake. His guilty conscience troubled him as he delivered her paper every morning, and she greeted him cheerfully. But he felt acutely uncomfortable, until he resolved on a plan of action – he would save his paper-round money and make it up to her for the cost of the broken window.

In a few weeks he had saved ten dollars which he had calculated would cover the cost of replacing the broken windowpane. He put the money inside an envelope, along with a note explaining that he was sorry for breaking her window, and was offering her the money to make up for the damage. The note was unsigned – he was still too scared to confess! Late in the evening, he walked up to her front door, slipped the envelope in her mailbox and came away quietly. He felt a terrible burden lifting away from his conscience, and felt that tomorrow, when she greeted him with her cheerful smile, he would be able to look her in the eye once again.

The next morning he delivered her paper and was able to return her warm smile and greeting. The lady said to him, "Wait a minute, Peter. I have something for you."

It was a bag of freshly baked cookies. Peter munched on the cookies contentedly as he walked home after the paper-route. As he took out another cookie, he caught sight of a note inside the bag. He took it out and was stunned to read the words – "I'm proud of you!"

The old lady had known all along that it was he who had broken the window. And yet she hadn't remonstrated, she hadn't pulled him up. She had continued to treat him with the same gentle kindness as before. And when he finally made amends, she had expressed her love and appreciation of his honesty! She was indeed a lady who knew how to love and forgive!

There was a couple – Edith and Carl Taylor. They loved each other with no ordinary love. Though they were not rich in the wealth of the world, just because of the love her husband showered upon her, Edith regarded herself as the luckiest woman in the town. She and Carl had been married 23 years, but it appeared as though they were newly married. Her heart still skipped a beat when Carl walked into the room. Carl, too, loved his wife. Whenever his work took him out of town, he would write to Edith a love-letter every night. He sent her small gifts from every place he visited.

In February 1950, the Government sent Carl to Okinawa for a few months to work in a new warehouse. (Carl worked in the Government Warehouse Department). This time, there were no daily letters and no gifts. Each time Edith enquired why Carl had been away for so long, he would write that he would have to stay another month or two. A year passed, but Carl did not return. His letters became less frequent and more formal and love was missing in them.

Then, after weeks of silence, a letter came, "Dear Edith, I wished there were a kinder way to tell you that I have applied to Mexico for a divorce. I want to marry a Japanese woman whom I love. Aiko is her name. She is a maid-of-all-work who has served me so well."

The first reaction was shock, then fury. Should she fight that quick paper-divorce? She hated her husband and that woman for having shattered her life. Hurt had let to hate and hate burnt within her. But the grace of God descended on Edith. Soon she arrived at the third stage – that of healing. She tried not to judge her husband but to understand his situation. He was a lonely man. His heart was full of love. Aiko was a penniless girl. Under these circumstances, it was so easy for a man and woman to come together. And Carl had not done a shameful thing. He had chosen the way of divorce rather than take advantage of a young servant girl. Aiko was 19 and Edith was 48. Edith wrote to Carl, asking him to keep in touch with her, to write to her, from time to time, giving her all the news.

One day, Carl wrote that he and Aiko were expecting a baby. She was born in 1951. She was named Marie. Then in 1953, another girl was born,

Helen. Edith sent gifts to the little girls. Carl and Edith continued to write to each other.

Edith had no interest in life. She just existed. She worked in a factory and earned a livelihood. She hoped that Carl would some day come back to her.

One day, she got a letter that Carl was dying of lung cancer. Carl's last letters were full of fear, not for himself but for Aiko and the two little girls. What would become of them? His entire savings were spent on paying hospital bills. He would die a penniless man.

It cost Edith a tremendous effort to take the decision. She loved Carl. What was there she could not do for the sake of that love! She wrote to Carl that if Aiko was willing, she would adopt Marie and Helen as her children. Edith realised that it would be hard, at the age of 54, to be a mother of two little children. "I shall do it for the sake of Carl," she decided.

Carl died. Edith looked after Marie and Helen. It was a hard job. She worked harder to earn a little more to feed the two extra mouths. She became ill, but she kept working because she was afraid of losing a day's salary. At the factory, one day, she fainted.

She was in the hospital for two weeks with pneumonia. There, in the hospital bed, her thoughts went out to Aiko. How lonely she must feel with her daughters away from her, her husband dead, her children in a foreign land. What must be Aiko's condition?

Edith took the final step on the path of forgiveness. The mother must come and be with the children. But there was the immigration problem. Aiko was a Japanese citizen. And the immigration quota had a waiting list many years long.

Edith wrote to an editor of a paper who described the situation in his newspaper. Petitions were started. A special bill speeded through the Congress and, in August 1957, Aiko was permitted to enter the United States.

As the plane arrived in New York's International Airport, Edith had a moment of fear. What if she should hate the woman who had taken Carl away from her. Aiko was the last passenger to leave the plane. She did not come down the stairs. She clutched the railing and stood there. Edith realised how panicky Aiko felt. Edith summoned up sufficient strength and called Aiko's name, and the girl rushed down the steps and into Edith's arms. In that brief moment, as they held each other, Edith prayed, "God, help me to love this girl as if she was a part of Carl come home. I prayed for him to come back. Now he is in his two little daughters and in the gentle girl that he loved. Help me, God, to know that!"

I will close the story with this simple question: my dear brothers and sisters, tell me, could you have loved as much as Edith loved?

Before Edith died, she repeated the words she used to utter when she and Carl lived together, "I am the luckiest woman in town!"

Forgiving those who hurt us is the key to personal peace.

G. Weatherly

Never does the human soul appear so strong and noble as when it foregoes revenge and dares to forgive an injury.

E. H. Chapin

Forgiveness is the strength of the weak and ornament of the strong.

– Chanakya

About the Author

Dada J.P. Vaswani's inspirational books have reached out to thousands of readers worldwide, communicating, as only he can, his practical, down-to-earth approach to life and living, helping people to overcome problems and challenges and make the most of the great gift that is human life!

Dada's philosophy is not theoretical – it is the art of daily living; his spirituality is not abstract – it consists simply of thinking good thoughts, speaking good words and doing good deeds; his God is love, his religion is service and sacrifice. Dada is the very embodiment of humility and love.

Dada ennobles and illumines everything he touches. His books have proved to be bestsellers, and have been translated into several languages in India and across the world.

Admired and revered as one of the outstanding spiritual leaders of modern India, Dada has reached out to the hearts and spirits of people wherever he has travelled. Dada's exciting, new books in the *Life Guides* Series, have been compiled from the inspiring, uplifting talks that he has delivered to enthralled audiences all over the world

Printed in the United States
73393LV00004B/496-507